CAMBRIDGE LIBRARY COLLECTION

Books of enduring scholarly value

Egyptology

The large-scale scientific investigation of Egyptian antiquities by Western scholars began as an unintended consequence of Napoleon's invasion of Egypt during which, in 1799, the Rosetta Stone was discovered. The military expedition was accompanied by French scholars, whose reports prompted a wave of enthusiasm that swept across Europe and North America resulting in the Egyptian Revival style in art and architecture. Increasing numbers of tourists visited Egypt, eager to see the marvels being revealed by archaeological excavation. Writers and booksellers responded to this growing interest with publications ranging from technical site reports to tourist guidebooks and from children's histories to theories identifying the pyramids as repositories of esoteric knowledge. This series reissues a wide selection of such books. They reveal the gradual change from the 'tomb-robbing' approach of early excavators to the highly organised and systematic approach of Flinders Petrie, the 'father of Egyptology', and include early accounts of the decipherment of the hieroglyphic script.

Methods and Aims in Archaeology

A pioneering Egyptologist, Sir William Matthew Flinders Petrie (1853–1942) excavated over fifty sites and trained a generation of archaeologists. In this short but classic work of 1904, he explains his vision for the young science of archaeology. Petrie outlines his processes and goals for an excavation, offering advice on how to manage workers drawn from the local population as well as guidance on creating a thorough record of a dig, the importance of which had not been fully appreciated by many contemporary archaeologists. His methods were highly influential in their more systematic and scientific approach to archaeology at a time when many of its practitioners were more focused on acquiring attractive artefacts than advancing knowledge. The text is accompanied by 66 illustrations. Petrie wrote prolifically throughout his long career, and a great many of his other publications – for both specialists and non-specialists – are also reissued in this series.

T0381842

Cambridge University Press has long been a pioneer in the reissuing of out-of-print titles from its own backlist, producing digital reprints of books that are still sought after by scholars and students but could not be reprinted economically using traditional technology. The Cambridge Library Collection extends this activity to a wider range of books which are still of importance to researchers and professionals, either for the source material they contain, or as landmarks in the history of their academic discipline.

Drawing from the world-renowned collections in the Cambridge University Library and other partner libraries, and guided by the advice of experts in each subject area, Cambridge University Press is using state-of-the-art scanning machines in its own Printing House to capture the content of each book selected for inclusion. The files are processed to give a consistently clear, crisp image, and the books finished to the high quality standard for which the Press is recognised around the world. The latest print-on-demand technology ensures that the books will remain available indefinitely, and that orders for single or multiple copies can quickly be supplied.

The Cambridge Library Collection brings back to life books of enduring scholarly value (including out-of-copyright works originally issued by other publishers) across a wide range of disciplines in the humanities and social sciences and in science and technology.

Methods and Aims
in Archaeology

W.M. FLINDERS PETRIE

CAMBRIDGE
UNIVERSITY PRESS

CAMBRIDGE
UNIVERSITY PRESS

University Printing House, Cambridge, CB2 8BS, United Kingdom

Published in the United States of America by Cambridge University Press, New York

Cambridge University Press is part of the University of Cambridge.
It furthers the University's mission by disseminating knowledge in the pursuit of
education, learning and research at the highest international levels of excellence.

www.cambridge.org
Information on this title: www.cambridge.org/9781108065979

© in this compilation Cambridge University Press 2013

This edition first published 1904
This digitally printed version 2013

ISBN 978-1-108-06597-9 Paperback

This book reproduces the text of the original edition. The content and language reflect
the beliefs, practices and terminology of their time, and have not been updated.

Cambridge University Press wishes to make clear that the book, unless originally published
by Cambridge, is not being republished by, in association or collaboration with, or
with the endorsement or approval of, the original publisher or its successors in title.

METHODS AND AIMS

IN

ARCHAEOLOGY

Fig. 1. CHAIN OF BOYS CLEARING THE OSIREION AT ABYDOS.
41 feet deep.

METHODS & AIMS

IN

ARCHAEOLOGY

BY

W. M. FLINDERS PETRIE

HON. D.C.L., LL.D., LIT.D., PH.D. : F.R.S. ; HON. F.S.A.(SCOT.) :

Member of the Imperial German Archaeological Institute ;
Member of the Society of Northern Antiquaries ;
Member of the Roman Society of Anthropology ;
Edwards Professor of Egyptology, University College, London.

WITH 66 ILLUSTRATIONS

London

MACMILLAN AND CO., Limited

NEW YORK : THE MACMILLAN COMPANY

1904

TO MY FRIENDS

F. LL. GRIFFITH,
E. A. GARDNER,
F. J. BLISS,
H. CARTER,
B. P. GRENFELL,
J. E. QUIBELL,
J. DUNCAN,
H. F. PETRIE,
N. DE O. DAVIES,
A. C. MACE,
D. RANDALL-MACIVER,
B. ORME,
A. E. WEIGALL,
M. A. MURRAY,
L. ECKENSTEIN,
H. STANNUS,
C. T. CURRELLY,
E. R. AYRTON,

WHO HAVE JOINED IN VARIOUS PORTIONS OF THE WORK HERE
DESCRIBED, 1884-1903.

PREFACE

ARCHAEOLOGY is the latest born of the sciences. It has but scarcely struggled into freedom, out of the swaddling clothes of dilettante speculations. It it still attracted by pretty things, rather than by real knowledge. It has to find shelter with the Fine Arts or with History, and not a single home has yet been provided for its real growth.

All other sciences deal with the things around us ; with subjects which may, or may not, affect us. Even medical sciences are concerned with the mechanical structure of the body, rather than with the nature and abilities of the mind. But the science which enquires into all the products and works of our own species, which shows what man has been doing in all ages and under all conditions, which reveals his mind, his thoughts, his tastes, his feelings, —such a science touches us more closely than any other.

By this science, of which History forms a part, we trace the nature of man, age after age,—his

capacities, his abilities ; we learn where he succeeds, where he fails, and what his possibilities
may be.

From another point of view the subject should be
considered ; it gives a more truly " liberal education "
than any other subject, as at present taught. A
complete archaeological training would require a full
knowledge of history and art, a fair use of languages,
and a working familiarity with many sciences. The
one-sided growth of modern training, which produces
a B.A. who knows nothing of natural science, or else
a B.Sc. who knows nothing of human nature, is
assuredly not the ideal for a reasonable man.
Archaeology,— the knowledge of how man has
acquired his present position and powers—is one of
the widest studies, best fitted to open the mind, and
to produce that type of wide interests and toleration
which is the highest result of education.

Though this volume is a book of reference for
those engaged in actual work, yet it will also serve
to give the public a view of the way in which this
work is done, the mode in which results are obtained,
the ends which are pursued, and the important
questions which must be considered. We have
nothing here to do with the details of the facts
discovered ; but deal only with the methods and aims,
which have been slowly learned in a quarter of a
century. Yet every year there are fresh methods to
add, and more clear views of the aims ; and far more

might easily have been said about each of the subjects here discussed.

If in this outline there is much more reference to Egypt than to other countries, it is for the reason that most of my own work has lain there ; and there is the more need to deal with that land, as more exploration is going on there than elsewhere.

I have to thank my friends for six of the photographs here used.

W. M. FLINDERS PETRIE.

University College, London.

CONTENTS

CHAPTER I

THE EXCAVATOR

CHAPTER II

DISCRIMINATION

CHAPTER III

THE LABOURERS

xi

CHAPTER IV

ARRANGEMENT OF WORK

CHAPTER V

RECORDING IN THE FIELD

CHAPTER VI

COPYING

CHAPTER VII

PHOTOGRAPHING

CHAPTER VIII

PRESERVATION OF OBJECTS

CONTENTS

CHAPTER IX

PACKING

CHAPTER X

PUBLICATION

CHAPTER XI

SYSTEMATIC ARCHAEOLOGY

CHAPTER XII

ARCHAEOLOGICAL EVIDENCE

CONTENTS

PAGE

148; Scarabs, 149; Tombs in Egypt, 150;
Tombs in Greece, 152; Variation with date, 153;
Style, 154; Recapitulation, 155; XIIth Dynasty,
Kahun, 156; XIIth Dynasty in Crete, 158;
Pan-graves, 159; VIth to IIIrd Dynasties, 162;
Ist Dynasty Aegean, 164; Ist Dynasty Cretan,
166; Prehistoric, 167   136–168

CHAPTER XIII

ETHICS OF ARCHAEOLOGY

Individual rights, 169; Destruction, 170; Restoration, 172; Sacrifices, 173; Responsibility, 174;
Rights of the future, 175; Rights of the past,
176; Duties, 178; Future of museums, 180;
Publications, 182; State claims, 183; State
rights, 184; Excavating laws, 187 .   .   . 169–188

CHAPTER XIV

THE FASCINATION OF HISTORY 189–193

INDEX   195–208

LIST OF ILLUSTRATIONS

Figs. 2, 3. GOING UP THE DESERT, ABYDOS.

CHAPTER I

THE EXCAVATOR

IN few kinds of work are the results so directly dependent on the personality of the worker as they are in excavating. The old saying that a man finds what he looks for in a *Purpose.* subject, is too true ; or if he has not enough insight to ensure finding what he looks for, it is at least sadly true that he does not find anything that he does not look for. Whether it be inscriptions, carvings, papyri, or mummies that excavators have been seeking, they have seldom preserved or cared for anything but their own limited object.

Of late years the notion of digging merely for profitable spoil, or to yield a new excitement to the jaded, has spread unpleasantly——at least in Egypt. A concession to dig is sought much like a grant of a monastery at the Dissolution : the man who has influence or push, a title or a trade connection, claims to try his luck at the spoils of the land. Gold digging has at least no moral responsibility, beyond the ruin of the speculator ; but spoiling the past has an acute moral wrong in it, which those who do it

B

may be charitably supposed to be too ignorant or unintelligent to see or realise.

And some systematic outline of archaeological methods and aims is needed, not only for those whose moral sense is so untrained that they may ruin a site, and say " I have done no wrong " ; but it may even profit those who take up the name of archaeology when they mean solely art, or inscriptions, or some single branch of the subject.   The most familiar teaching entitled archaeological is that of Classical Archaeology, which in the ways of most teachers means Greek sculpture and vase paintings. In spite of all the professorships and schools of that subject, we are still so profoundly ignorant of the archaeology of Greece and Italy that there is scarcely a single class of common objects of which any one knows the history and transformations.   Certainly we know far less of the archaeology of classical lands than we do of that of Egypt.

If, then, the character of the excavator thus determines his results, our first step is to consider

Character.

that character, and to give some outline of the aptitudes and acquirements—the wit and the cunning, as our forefathers well distinguished them—which are wanted in order to avoid doing more harm than good.

Firstly in every subject there is the essential division between those who work to live, and those who live to work—the commercial, and the scientific or artistic aim ;—those who merely do what will best provide them a living, and those whose work is their honour and the end of their being.   These two halves of mankind are by no means to be found ready labelled by their professions. The R.A. who drops his aspirations because portraits pay best, the scientific scholar who patents every invention he can, are of the true commercial spirit, and verily they have their reward. Rather let us honour the professed dealer who will sooner sell a group to a museum than make a larger profit by playing to the wealthy *dilettante* and scattering things. Let us be quit, in archaeology at least, of the brandy-and-soda young man who manipulates his "expenses," of the adventurous speculator, of those who think that a title or a long purse glorifies any vanity or selfishness.

Without the ideal of solid continuous work, certain, accurate, and permanent,—archaeology is as futile as any other pursuit. Money alone will not do the work; brains are the first requisite. A hundred pounds intelligently spent will do more good and far less harm than ten thousand squandered in doing damage. Mere money gives no moral right to upset things according to the whim of one person. Even scholarship is by no means all that is wanted; the engineering training of mind and senses which Prof. Perry advocates will really fit an archaeologist better for excavating than book-work can alone. Best of all is the combination of the scholar and the engineer, the man of languages and the man of physics and mathematics, when such can be found. So much for the wit, and now of the cunning that is wanted.

The most needful of all acquisitions is archaeological experience. Without knowing well all the objects that are usually met with in an ancient civilisation, there is no possible Experience. insight or understanding, the meaning of what is met with cannot be grasped, and the most curious mistakes are made. A cloud is " very like a whale," the pre-Christian cross is found everywhere, an arrow-straightener is called a ceremonial staff, an oil-press becomes a sacred trilithon, half a jackal is called a locust, and lathe chucks become " coal money." Of course the needed experience has to be gradually built up, and those who first explore a civilisation must work through many mistakes. When I first came to Egypt Dr. Birch begged me to pack and send to him a box of pottery fragments from each great town, on the chance that from the known history of the sites some guess could be made as to the age of the objects ; so complete was the ignorance of the archaeology a quarter of a century ago. But when such knowledge has been once accumulated, it is the first duty of any excavator to make himself well acquainted with it before he attempts to discover more. At present the archaeological experience that should be acquired before doing any responsible work in any country ought to cover the history of the pottery century by century, the history of beads, of tools and weapons, of the styles of art, of the styles of inscriptions, of the burial furniture, and of the many small objects which are now well known and dated, better in Egypt than perhaps in any other country.

Next to this is needed a good knowledge of the history. Not only every dynasty, but every king of whom anything is known, should be familiar. The general course of the civilisation, the foreign influences which affected the country, and the conditions at different periods, should be clearly in mind. Without such ideas the value and meaning of discoveries cannot be grasped, and important clues and fresh knowledge may be passed by.

Organization, both of the plan of work, and of the labourers, is very necessary. Scheming how to extract all that is possible from a given site, how to make use of all the condi-tions, how to avoid difficulties; and training labourers, keeping them all firmly in hand, making them all friends without allowing familiarity, getting their full confidence and their goodwill;—these requirements certainly rank high in an excavator's outfit.

Organization.

The power of conserving material and informa-tion ; of observing all that can be gleaned ; of noticing trifling details which may imply a great deal else; of acquiring and building up a mental picture ; of fitting everything into place, and not losing or missing any possible clues ;—all this is the soul of the work, and without it excavating is mere dumb plodding.

Acquirements.

Of more external subjects, such as may be deputed to other helpers, drawing is mainly wanted ; more in mechanical exactitude of facsimile-copying than in freehand or purely artistic work. Surveying and practical mathematics, with plan drawing, are almost always involved in dealing with any site. Photo-graphy is incessantly in use, both during the course of the working and for preparing publications. The outlines of chemistry and physics and a good know-ledge of materials are necessary to avoid blunders in handling objects and in describing them. The ancient language of a country, all important as it is in the study of remains, is yet in its critical aspects not so essential during field-work. But the excavator should at least be able to take the sense of all written material which he finds ; and in Egypt that should include hieroglyphic, hieratic, demotic, Greek, and Coptic writing. The spoken language of the country should be fluently acquired for simple purposes, so as to be able to direct workmen, make bargains, and follow what is going on. To be dependent on a cook, a dragoman, or a donkey boy, is very unsafe, and prevents that close study of the workmen which is needed for making the best use of them. And a general eye to the safety and condition of everything, both of work, antiquities, and stores, is incessantly wanted if a camp is to be successful and prosperous.

Many of these requirements can well be under-taken by different people ; in fact, not a single living person combines all of the requisite qualities for complete archaeological work. But all of these requirements must be fulfilled by different members in a party, if they are to command success as well as deserve it. In all points, imagination and insight, the sense of all the possibilities of a case, is to be the medium of thought both in theoretical and in practical affairs.

In the externals of the work an excavator should be always his own best workman. If he be the **Demands of the work.** strongest on the place, so much the better ; but at all events he should be the most able in all matters of skill and ability. Where anything is found it should be the hands of the master that clear it from the soil ; the pick and the knife should be in his hands every day, and his readiness should be shown by the shortness of his

CAMP LIFE, ABYDOS.

Fig. 4. Tent in desert. | Fig. 5. Huts at temple.

finger-nails and the toughness of his skin. After a
week of work in the soil, feeling for delicate things
in a way that no tools can do, the skin almost wears
through, and the nails break down. But a week or
two more at it, and the excavator grows his gloves,
and is in a fit state for business, with the skin well
thickened, and ready to finger through tons of
grit and sand. Nothing can be a substitute for
finger-work in extracting objects, and clearing ground
delicately ; and one might as well try to play the
violin in a pair of gloves as profess to excavate with
clean fingers and a pretty skin. It need hardly be
said that clothing must correspond to the work ; and
there must never be a thought about clothes when
one kneels in wet mud, scrapes through narrow
passages, or sits waist deep in dust. To attempt
serious work in pretty suits, shiny leggings, or
starched collars, would be like mountaineering in
evening dress, or remind one of the old prints of
cricketers batting in chimney-pot hats. The man
who cannot enjoy his work without regard to appearances, who will not strip and go into the water, or
slither on slimy mud through unknown passages,
had better not profess to excavate. Alongside of
his men he must live, in work hours and out ; every
workman should come to him at all times for help
and advice. His courtyard must be the pay office
and the court of appeal for every one ; and continual
attention should be freely given to the many little
troubles of those who are to be kept properly in
hand. To suppose that work can be controlled
from a distant hotel, where the master lives in state
and luxury completely out of touch with his men, is

a fallacy, like playing at farming or at stockbroking :
it may be amusing, but it is not business.   And
whatever is not businesslike in archaeology is a waste
of the scanty material which should be left for those
who know how to use it.   An excavator must make
up his mind to do his work thoroughly and truly,
or else to leave it alone for others who will take the
trouble which it deserves and requires.

TEMPLE RUINS.

Fig. 6 El Hibeh.   Fig. 7. Tanis, with obelisks.

CHAPTER II

DISCRIMINATION

THE observing of resemblances and differences, and the memory of physical appearances required for this, are absolute requisites for carrying on the duties of excavating. Here we deal with the appearances in a land of sun-dried brickwork, where the accumulations are great, as in Egypt, Syria, and Mesopotamia. In a rocky land, such as Greece, there is not the same sheltering mud, and the appearances are therefore very different.

The nature of a site can be guessed pretty closely from its aspect. A wide open space with mounds around it is almost certainly a temple site ; and if there are stone chips strewn over it, no doubt remains as to its nature (Figs. 6, 7). The temples being of stone from the XIIth Dynasty onwards, they were ruined by the removal of the material in each age of disruption ; but the houses of the towns, being always of mud brick, continually crumbled and decayed, and so filled up the ground with rubbish. In Egypt mud-brick towns accumulate at about 20 inches in a century ; or in the rainy Syrian climate at about 50 inches. Herodotus describes walking on the roofs of the houses and

<section marker>Temples.</section marker>

seeing down into the temple precincts ; and in every
great site in Egypt, such as Tanis, Buto, Bubastis,
Memphis, or Koptos, the plain of temple ruins had
the house mounds far above it on all sides.   The
temples were ruined both for building-stone and for
lime-burning.   It is rare to get any portions of a
limestone building left ; sandstone is often found,
and all the great temples which remain are of sandstone ; granite generally has lasted, except where it
has been split up in Roman times for millstones.
The search for limestone has led to whole buildings
being upset in order to extract the limestone founda-
tions.   The basalt pavement of Khufu, the granite
pylon of Crocodilopolis, and probably the granite
temple of Iseum, have been overthrown thus.
Especially in the Delta, where no limestone hills are
accessible, this destructive search for lime has been
unrelenting in all ages ; and it is seldom that
ancient limestone is now met with.   Hence all that
can generally be seen of a temple site is a plain of
dust with a few tumbled blocks of granite, the exposed tops of which are entirely weathered as
rounded masses.   Five. or ten feet down there may
be a rich harvest of carvings and inscriptions.

A town site is always recognised (Fig. 8) by its
mounds of crumbling mud brick, strewn with potsherds if in Upper Egypt, or with burnt
red bricks on the later mounds of the
Delta.   Whenever a native begins to describe a site
in Lower Egypt, one inquires if there is red brick,
and if so there is no need to listen further. Generally
it is possible to date the latest age of a town by the
potsherds lying on the surface ; and to allow a rate

Towns.

Fig. 8. Mounds of fort, Defeneh. | Fig. 9. Sarcophagi at Zuweleyn.

of growth of 20 inches a century down to the visible
level ; if that gives a long period we may further
carry down the certainly artificial level by 4 inches
in a century for the Nile deposits when in the
cultivated ground.   For instance, there are mounds
in the Delta about 40 feet high, ending about
500 A.D. ; this gives about 40 feet of rise, equal to
about 2400 years, or say 2000 B.C., for the age at
the present ground level.   But the visible base was
about 5 feet lower at 500 A.D. ; and the human
deposit rising at 20 inches a century has been over-
laid at the rate of 4 inches a century by the Nile
deposit.   Hence the age may be reckoned by a
depth of 45 feet accumulated at 16 inches a century
before 500 A.D. or about 2900 B.C.   No exact
conclusion could be based on this ; but it is a
valuable clue to the age to which the yet unseen
foundation of a town may most likely belong.
Town mounds and ruins of buildings have generally
symmetrical forms, weathered away uniformly on all
sides.   But around towns are often heaps of rubbish
thrown out, the best-known example of this being
the immense heaps behind Cairo ; and such accumulations usually show their nature by the two
slopes, the gradual walk-up slope, and the steep
thrown-down slope.

The cemetery sites on the desert have always
been more or less plundered anciently.   A prehistoric site may have no external   Cemeteries.
trace, as the blown sand may cover it
so evenly that there is no suspicion of anything
lying beneath.   But on a gravel surface there are
generally some indications left of the hollows of the

graves, and scraps of broken pottery left about by the plunderers (Fig. 9). The historic cemeteries are generally easier to see, as they are in rising ground, and the holes of the tomb pits show on the surface. The difficulty is not to find the site of a cemetery, but to find a grave in it which still contains anything. As a rule, any tomb pit which appears still undisturbed has been left either because it belongs to an unfinished tomb with nothing in it, or because the tomb has already been reached from elsewhere. At Medum an untouched walling up of a chamber had been left, because the plunderers had tunnelled under the mass of the tomb and broken through the floor of the chamber. At Dendereh the floor of the chamber was entire, with the lid of the sarcophagus sunk in it, yet untouched; it had been left so because the plunderers had mined through from the outside under the floor to the sarcophagus, and broken through the side of it without touching the chamber. Some untouched tombs were left because the burials in them were known to be so poor that they were not worth opening. All this points to the plundering being mostly done during the lifetime of those who saw the burial. Usually only one tomb in ten contains anything noticeable; and it is only one in a hundred that repays the digging of the other ninety-nine.

In general, on looking over a site every indication must be observed. Sometimes there may be a slight

Indications. difference in vegetation, showing the positions of walls or of pits. In colder climates differences are shown by the melting of hoar frost or snow; as in the square of S. Domenico at

Bologna, where some large patches—probably of ashes—show through the cobble paving during a thaw. A shower of rain will show much in drying; and, after a rare storm in Egypt, there are two or three precious hours when the buried walls show clearly on the ground, and should be hurriedly scored down before the hot sun removes the traces. A driving wind will bare the ground so that the harder walls show through the sand; or even a crowd of people passing will tramp into the softer filling and show the constructions. At sunrise or sunset ground should be carefully looked over to pick out the variations of level and slope, which will often show then, though quite invisible in full light. Prehistoric camp sites are noticed by the difference of tone of the ground in walking over them; the ashes holding so much air that the reverberation to the foot-step is quite different from that on ordinary desert. The appearance of the surface of disturbed desert differs much from the undisturbed: there may be slight hollows filled with sand, which are the traces of deep pits; there may be pebbles from deep beds thrown up, or fragments of limestone; or—best of all—chips of worked stone or of hard rocks may tell the tale of a building whose ruins lie beneath. The mastabas of the XIIth Dynasty at Dahshur left scarcely any surface trace, as the stone walls had been removed, and the gravel filling had spread out and denuded down to a level surface. The great wall of the camp at Daphnae 40 feet thick, had been ploughed by denudation until it was even lower than the desert on either side of it, and the lines of it were only visible by the absence of potsherds upon the site of the wall.

Besides the discrimination of sites there is a vast subject in the discrimination of objects and of styles.
Productions. The first requisite acquirement of a digger—his archaeological experience—consists in discriminating and distinguishing the differences between products of various dates. An Egyptian copper adze (Fig. 10). of the ages of middle prehistoric, late prehistoric, early dynastic, IIIrd,

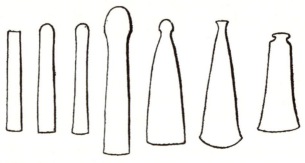

Mid, Late, Prehistoric.   Ist,   IIIrd,   VIth,   XIIth,   XVIIIth Dyn.

Fig. 10.—Development of copper and bronze adzes. 1 : 6.

VIth, XIIth, or XVIIIth Dynasties can be told at a glance, and we only need more dated examples to be able to separate them still more finely. A cutting-out knife (Fig. 11), a pair of tweezers, a comb, can be dated almost as certainly. But it is when we can look not only to differences of form, but also to variations of colour and texture, that we have the widest scope for discrimination. The great variety of beads in each country, the hundreds of details of form, materials, and colour in Egypt alone, give them an importance archaeologically above most other things. In the prehistoric age there are a dozen materials, and many different forms, not one of which can be confounded with later products. In the Old Kingdom new and distinctive styles are met with, and a profusion of small amulets on necklaces. In the XIth and XIIth Dynasties magnificent beads of amethyst, green felspar, and carnelian outshine those of every other age. In the XVIIIth Dynasty the

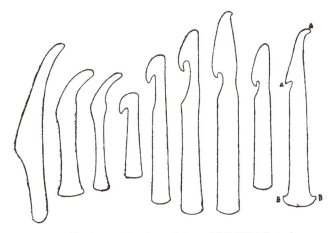

FIG 11.—Development of cutting-out knives. XIIth-XIXth Dynasties.
A–A and B–B cutting edges.

immense variety of glass and glazed beads defy enumeration, and yet are sharply characteristic of different reigns of that age. The later times of degradation also produce new and distinctive forms and colours ; and when we reach the Roman period a flood of glass work imitates the fashionable beryl, amethyst, rock crystal, and other stones, with the mimicry of a forger.

Pottery is, however, the greatest resource of the

archaeologist. For variety of form and texture, for
decoration, for rapid change, for its quick
fall into oblivion, and for its incomparable

Pottery.

abundance, it is in every respect the most important
material for study (Fig. 12), and it constitutes the

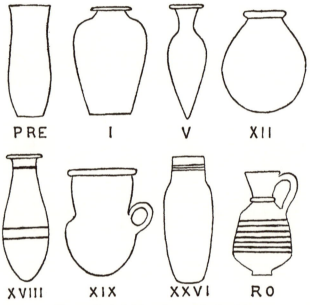

PRE   I   V   XII

XVIII   XIX   XXVI   RO

FIG. 12.—One typical form of pottery of each period.

essential alphabet of archaeology in every land.
Think for a moment how few people know the
appearance of a common jug a century old, how the
crocks of Georgian times have all vanished, and new
forms are made. Even of decorated china not one
piece in a thousand in England is before the last
century, and not one in a million is three centuries

old ; so rapidly does breakable ware perish, and
become unknown. This not only prevents its being
handed on from earlier times, as ornaments or weapons
may descend, but it prevents the copying of older
forms, and gives a free scope to rapid variation. No
doubt some standard forms may continue to be
made, because they are so simple, and so adapted to
common wants, that the same causes continue to
produce them. But it is only the simplest and least
characteristic types which thus continue ; the more
detailed and specialised the form, the more rapidly it
changes, and gives way to new styles. In the
prehistoric age of Egypt alone there are about a
thousand different forms of pottery ; and when the
historic times shall be as fully recorded, probably two
or three times as many will demand notice. In Italy
and Greece there is apparently as great a variety,
though—apart from painted vases—it is very far
from being fully placed on paper. And when we
come to know the archaeology of other lands, their
pottery will doubtless prove as varied and distinctive
in its styles. It is then in a thorough knowledge of
pottery that any sound archaeology must be based ;
and there is no wider or more important field for discrimination. With the brief view of Palestinian pottery
gained in a few weeks, on one site at Tell Hesy (Lach-
ish), I found it possible to ride over mounds of ruins
and see the age of them without even dismounting.

Beside the discrimination of broad physical differences there is the more subtle observation of style.
This cannot be discussed, or even shown
to exist, without a very wide collection of   Style.
examples ; yet in a trained observer a long series of

C

experience should result in an unexpressed—almost intangible and incommunicable—sense of the style of each country and each age, such that a piece of work can at once be referred to its proper place, though not a single exact comparison can be quoted for it. Special motives, outlines, curves, tastes, belong to various sources so certainly and characteristically that they show their origin at a glance. A good example of this is seen in the bronzes of Minusinsk in Central Asia ; this site is almost equidistant from the North Sea, the Persian Gulf, and the China Sea, and the style seems to recall by its details almost equally the taste of Northmen, Persians, and Chinese. A good practice for such discrimination is the analysis of common ornament around us : a rug or a wall pattern may be analysed into its sources—here a bit from Assyria, there from Egypt, here from Japan, there from Norway, all hashed together by the modern designer. And until the common and obviously distinctive patterns of each country can be named at sight, and separated into their various sources, the observer cannot hope to gain that far more essential sense of the national taste of each people, and the sympathetic feeling of the relationship of any form or curve that may chance to be seen,—that conviction of the family and source of each object, which is the illumination of an archaeologist, the guide to fresh suggestions and researches, the mental framework which holds all memories in place.

But beside this sublimated use of the permanent memory and discrimination, there is another very crude and transient discrimination which is also needed in actual work. A visual memory of the site and excavations should be constantly in mind ; the master should be able to go over the whole site, and every man at work on it, *Visual Memory.* entirely from memory ; he should be able to realise at once, on seeing the place next day, exactly how every one of fifty different holes looked the day before ; and know at once where the work stood, and what has been done since, so as to measure it up without depending on any statements by the workmen. If a boy comes with a message that Ibrahim or Mutwali needs direction, the master should be able to visualise the place, inquire what has been done, and how each part now stands, and then give sufficient temporary direction entirely from memory of the site, and memory of what he expected to do, or to prove, or to find, from that particular 'hole. The extent of this visual memory is never realised until one meets with some who are so unlucky as not to possess such an apparatus, and who are therefore unable to know what has been done, and have to begin each day's work as if they were strangers to the place. Of all inherent mental qualifications there is perhaps none more essential to a digger than this permanent picture of a site in the mind. And the transient memory from day to day should include the appearance of every hole on all sides, the meaning of it and the purpose for which it is being dug.

CHAPTER III

THE LABOURERS

In starting an excavation one of the first consider-
ations is the supply of labourers, and the selection of
them. In some places it is difficult to
Quality. persuade any one to work at first ; either
from distrust, or from being unaccustomed to regular
employment. At Naukratis only a few men could
be persuaded to try the work in the first week or
two ; but so soon as the villagers found that genuine
gold coin was to be had, they swarmed up, and some
five hundred demanded to be taken. The Egyptian
is good at steady work, but the Syrian is very
different, and it took some weeks at Tell Hesy to
educate men into continuous regular digging. They
would jump out of their holes every few minutes,
and squat on the edge for a talk with the next
man ; and only a steady weeding out of about a third
of them every week, gradually brought up the best
of them into tolerable efficiency. In Greece such
difficulties are even greater, and rational regular hard
work cannot be reckoned upon, as in Egypt.

The best age for diggers is about 15 to 20 years.
After that many turn stupid, and only a small pro-

Figs. 13, 14. WORKERS AT TANIS.

portion are worth having between 20 and 40. After 40 very few are of any use, though some robust men will continue to about 50. The Egyptian ages early; and men of 45 would be supposed to be 65 in England. The boys are of use for carrying from about 10 years old; and they generally look mere boys till over 20. The ornamental man with a good beard is quite useless and lazy; and the best workers are the scraggy under-sized youths, with wizened wiry faces, though sometimes a well-favoured lad with pleasing face will turn out very good (Fig. 13). In choosing boys the broad face and square chin are necessary tokens of stamina; and the narrow feminine faces are seldom worth much.

Beside the mere physical strength of the fellow, the face has to be studied for the character. The only safe guide in selecting workers is the expression; and no influence of recommendations or connections should weigh in the least against the judgment of the appearance. The qualities to be considered are, first, the honesty, shown mostly by the eyes, and by a frank and open bearing; next, the sense and ability; and lastly, the sturdiness, and freedom from nervous weakness and hysterical tendency to squabble.

When once selected, the education of the workers begins. Often some oafs who will not understand any directions, and have no sense to work unless encouraged by watching, may Education. yet be brought up in a few months to be good workers if associated with a skilful man. And almost every boy and man will greatly improve by steady work and control. The effect of selection and training is astonishingly seen on comparing some old hands, who have had five or ten years at the business, side by side with new lads.   There is as much differ-ence between their capacities as there is between the fellah and an educated Englishman.   A gang of well-trained men need hardly any direction, especially in cemetery work ; and their observations and know-ledge should always be listened to, and will often determine matters.   The freshman from England is their inferior in everything except in recording ; and at least a season's experience is needed before any one can afford to disregard the judgment of a well-trained digger.   The better class of these workers are one's personal friends, and are regarded much as old servants are in a good household.   Their feelings and self-respect must be thought of, as among our own equals, and they will not put up with any rudeness or contempt.   A man with landed property and cattle, and an ancestry of a couple of centuries, can afford to look down on most Englishmen who would bully him.   Such workers are of course entirely above going into the usual Government or French work, where the lash is used ; and their good service and skill is only given for friendly treatment.

Yet there is a danger in letting control slip away. It is always needful to be firm, and to insist on **Control.**   obedience to orders ; and constant keep-ing in hand is required, not only for the rank and file but even for the best men.   An Egyptian cannot withstand temptations if often repeated ; and the fault of a collapse of character, which befalls even the best, is mainly due to not keeping sufficient hold and influence, and not taking sufficient trouble to ensure control.   The first rule

in managing the better class of men is not to let
any man get a habit or prerogative of doing any
kind of work for oneself : never let the same man
repeatedly go for purchases, or for money, or carry
things, or walk with the master, or explain phrases,
or boss anybody or anything.   All such services
should be carefully spread over several men ; and if
there be two parties—as from opposite sides of the
Nile—always keep them well balanced in your consideration.   Each will then keep a sharp lookout on
the opposition.

Beside men and boys, girls (Fig. 15) will work
very well in the Delta and in Syria, though not in
Upper Egypt.   They do well at carrying ; and as
they never ask for pick work they are, when well
grown, worth more than the boys.   Not only will
they come from the village day by day, but they
will also camp out with their fathers and brothers in
camps at a distance from home.   No difficulty or
unpleasantness has arisen in such mixed camps in
my work.

A frequent trouble is from substitution of workers.
The fact of being chosen is worth something ; and
the worker will try to sell his place to a Substitutions.
substitute, and then get in again soon
after on the plea of being an old hand.   So long
as a substitute comes only for a day or so, he may
be tolerated.   But if there arises a frequent plea of
" So-and-So is ill to-day, and wants me to work for
him," it is needful to stamp on it by refusing all
substitutes, and replying, " If he is ill, I will take him
back when he is better."   One common cause is
that they wish to push in younger and younger

boys (Fig. 16), so that the fellow who was 14 or
16 at first, dwindles imperceptibly until he can
hardly carry a basket. An opposite cause is that
only boys are taken on in some places because the
men cannot be trusted; and then the supreme
object of the villains of the place is to get in as
substitutes for boys, so that they may learn what is
found and where to plunder at night. Most usually
when a substitute is refused the original boy turns
up as well as ever. I have known the village guards
come and call a lad out on a trumped-up charge,
with a friend of the guard following close by, quite
ready just to work for the accused.

Turning now to the organization, there are two
great choices to be made, with or without Overseers,
and by Day pay or Piecework. Each
Overseers. system may be best under particular
conditions, and the suitability of each we will note
first, before entering on detail.

Overseers are almost always employed. They
remove much of the friction; they profess to drive
the men on, and be responsible for their regular
working; and they seem indispensable parts of the
business. The less a master knows of the men and
of their language the more essential an overseer
seems to be.

Yet all this usefulness is the best reason for
avoiding them. The more friction they save, the
less the master knows of his men, and the less
influence he has. The more they profess to drive
the men, the more hollow the fraud is, until the
overseer merely serves to give notice when the
master is coming. The more indispensable they

Figs. 15, 16. GIRLS AND BOYS IN THE WORK.

seem, the less desirable is it to have so to trust a
native. And the less a master knows of the men
and the language, the more dangerous it is to have
some one always acting in everything that goes on.
Moreover, there is nothing so demoralising to a
native as wandering about, without hard work, stick
in hand, to bully men who are quite as good as
himself. Even good men soon lose their character
in such conditions, and it is needful to have some
definite allotted manual work for even a leading
man.

The results of having overseers, or *reises*, are
instructive. In one case the reis took a third of all
the money given as rewards for things, threatening
to get any man dismissed who would not give this
up to him. In another case the overseers levied a
sixth of all the wages from the men, making ten
times their own pay by this extortion. Mariette's
overseers used to go to a village with a Government
order for so many men, and demand the best men
they could venture on claiming. These bought
themselves off, each at a few shillings a month, and
lower men were taken, until most of the villagers
were paying heavy tribute. Reises will also bargain
with a shopkeeper to put on a third on the price of
all goods supplied, and compel any messenger sent
shopping to go to that shop. In another case a
museum reis was seen bowing down to the ground
and kissing the hand of the principal *antika*-dealer
of the place; doubtless for good consideration received. In short, the dangers, losses, and troubles
that come from reises are so great that it is far
better to do without them.

The system which works best is to have a careful distribution of the best men ; and, in fact, work with two or three dozen reises, all of whom do pick-work themselves. Each well-trained man can have half-a-dozen new hands placed near him, and he can be ordered to see that they follow instructions. By such a wide distribution of the authority it does not deteriorate the men, as there are too many rivals; and being each paid for actual digging, they do not spoil with idleness. Thus every man is directly under the master, all instructions are given at first hand, and every one is in close touch, and not fenced off by intermediate intriguers. Doubtless, two or three men will come to the front by their ability and character; but though full use should be made of them, yet they should always be kept nominally on the same terms and work as every one else. Their reward consists in being given all the more promising places, where things are likely to be found, so that they may reap much more profit than others.

Direct system.

In some different conditions of work overseers may be a necessary evil. In Greece the large distances of sites from each other in the Aegean and political conditions are a bar to employing a regular gang of men, although the Egyptian will readily travel three or four hundred miles to his season's work, as far as Constantinople from Athens, and is quite ready to do his work in spite of the scowls of a bad neighbourhood. Fresh workers are engaged at each place in Greece, and for their needful train-ing overseers are considered necessary. Also at present, owing to the continual shifting of European superintendence by changes of students, and less frequent changes of Directors, permanent overseers who will carry on the traditions of the modes of working are requisite.   But it is questionable whether these needs would not be more safely met by carrying about ten or a dozen picked workmen, who would train local hands, and at the same time work themselves.   The Greek does not seem nearly as capable of continuous hard work as is the Egyptian, and moves much less earth in the day, and that at about double the wages, while he is said to entirely refuse piecework.   But this difficulty would be reduced if a small picked body of hard workers, stimulated by good piece pay, were used as a nucleus to set the tone of steady work at each place.   The Greek needs educating to regular work, which is foreign to his nature.

In England about as much work may be done per man as in Egypt, but at about five or six times the cost.   Hence the number employed is not so large, twenty or thirty being a large gang, instead of 150 or 200 as in Egypt.   As they can follow directions tolerably, an overseer or foreman is not needed, the best of the workers usually taking the lead.

The question between Day pay and Piece pay is an open one.   In cases where minute valuables may be scattered anywhere in the soil, day pay is needful to prevent undue hurry.   Day pay. Or where the work is very irregular, and time needs to be spent on moving stones, or heavy extras, day pay must be given.   But where the work is uniform, and the objects expected are large or in known positions, then piecework is far more suitable. Though measuring up the cubic metres of work done may take perhaps a quarter of the master's time, yet that is better than having to give the whole time to spurring on the dawdling pace of day workers.

When working by the day it is needful to give the signals for beginning and stopping work, and to insist on regular and continuous digging. It is impossible to be known to be away, as then no work will go on effectively. An air of vigilant surprises has to be kept up. A sunk approach to the work behind higher ground is essential; and, if possible, an access to a commanding view without being seen going to and fro. A telescope is very useful to watch if distant work is regular. At Tanis the girls in a big pit were kept by the men walking up and tipping baskets at the top; but the telescope showed that the baskets were all the time empty. The immediate dismissal of fourteen people was the result. A telescope will also show if a boy is put up to watch for the master's coming. Various approaches should be arranged from different directions, and the course of work so planned that no men can give notice to others. In this way a pleasing group of musicians and dancers may be found in the excavations, where picks and baskets are lying idle; and the arrangement is closed by requesting the boys to dance on their own resources, and the transfer of your pay to other pockets. The need of thus acting as mainspring, without which the work goes on at an official pace, is wearing and time-wasting; and it leaves no chance of doing writing, drawing, etc., during work hours.

Working by the piece saves all this trouble, and
if the men are well trained, and the work is simple,
it goes on automatically and takes the
smallest possible amount of attention. Piecework.
In detached small sites men may even be left un-
visited for two or three days, merely reporting each
evening how far they have worked. In one case
some lads were left to work at a great sarcophagus
for weeks unwatched, and came some miles to report
progress, and say when further attention was wanted.
The pay for that was given by contract, to cut and
lift a stone lid under water, for so many pounds.

In piecework it is always best to keep a record of
how long each piece has taken, as the time is one
element in pricing the work done.[1] The ground
varies in hardness, the depth of throwing up continually changes, or the presence of large stones
hinders the work ; therefore any exact value by a
hard and fast rule is impossible. Each piece of
work done has to be judged, taking the most likely
scale of payment, and then tempering the result by
the amount of time occupied. The general rate of
pay in Egypt is $\frac{1}{2}$ piastre a cubic metre for loose
surface sand, $\frac{2}{3}$ for shallow work in harder earth, $\frac{3}{4}$
for work as deep as a man, and 1 piastre for deep
pits. At this scale a poor worker will barely earn
day pay and a fine worker will make from $1\frac{1}{2}$ to 2
times day pay. The day pay in Upper Egypt is $2\frac{1}{2}$
to 3 piastres (6d. to 7d.) a man, and $1\frac{1}{2}$ to 2 ($3\frac{1}{2}$d.
to 5d.) for a boy, of fit and proper quality.

---

[1] A useful notation is to use the letter of the week day, with an
hour-spot by it ; thus F is 7 A.M. Friday, M is 2 P.M. Monday, W
is noon, Wednesday, and this spotted letter is noted in the accounts, for
the time of beginning any piece of work.

To take a practical case. A hole is, say, $2\frac{1}{2}$ metres wide, $3\frac{1}{2}$ long and 2 deep, say 18 cubic metres. The rate will be at $\frac{3}{4}$, making $13\frac{1}{2}$ piastres or 2s. 9d. Large stones met with, or pillars or buttresses of earth left to support objects *in situ*, are counted as work done, as the trouble and inconvenience of leaving them in the hole is quite equal to the removal of so much earth. If the pit above-named had taken a four-gang (two men and two boys) less than a day, it might be cut to 12 piastres or 2s. 6d. ; or if much over a day, it might be raised to 16 or 3s. 3d. ; reckoning that a rate much quicker or slower than the regular rate, shows that the ground or conditions were better or worse than usual. It is needful to measure with distinct and visible care, as the men are very watchful to see that they get fair measurement ; and their confidence should be gained by taking trouble to be fair and punctilious in every detail, though never taking notice of any wheedling or attempt to influence the account.

Where the earth has to be moved to any distance beyond a few yards, then more carriers are needed Day and than one to each digger. The happiest Piecework. combination then is to go on paying exactly the same rate by the metre, as if the men were working a plain pit, but to supply them with as many boys paid by the day as may be needful to shift the earth away (Fig. 17). Sometimes two men and two boys will have six more boys to run off the earth to fifty yards away. Any common village boys will do for this gang, and they may be enlisted by the hundred, and distributed over the work. But

CLEARING THE TEMPLE, ABYDOS.

Fig. 17. Lines of carriers. | Fig. 18. Heaps around area.

it is needful to allot these "locals" (as they are
called) specifically to known men, so that each pick-
man can answer for the time and the doings of each
of his own boys.   Thus there is no smudge of irre-
sponsibility ; but each boy belongs to a man, who
has for his own interest to get the work out of him.

The local boys should all give the names of their
villages on enlistment, and be kept in lists according
to villages, so as to group them for payment in gold.
In case of any serious theft or trouble due to boys
from one village, all the rest from that village can be
dismissed as a warning.   To keep them up to time
in arriving, it is best to dismiss for the day the two
or three who come latest, if they are not well up to
time.   This soon enforces regularity.   Any attempt
to leave before the sunset signal, is met by dismissing
altogether any boy who leaves too soon.   It is best
not to allow any substitution on the plea of illness,
as if that is once allowed, it soon becomes a loophole for all the selected boys to gradually sell their
places to less desirable fellows.   A favourite plan of
the piecework men is to turn all their own basket-
boys into pick-boys, and then want more locals to
carry the stuff.   Of course this has to be met by
deducting from the rate of pay, as the regular rates
are for cutting and throwing, and not for cutting
alone.   The proportion of pay if the boys are set to
do pick-work, on a gang of two men and two boys,
goes as follows :—

[TABLE

pick 3	pick 3	pick 3
basket 2	pick 3	pick 3
pick 3	pick 3	pick 3
basket 2	basket 2	pick 3
A 10	B 11	C 12
	2 baskets due } 4	4 baskets due } 8
	15	20

Then if in a normal four-gang, A, one boy takes a pick they become as in B, and only have $\frac{11}{15}$ of the piece pay, as the master has to supply the other two baskets for the normal gang of equal numbers of picks and baskets.   Similarly if both boys take picks, as in C, the pay is of course $\frac{3}{5}$ of what it would normally be; the other $\frac{2}{5}$ being spent in supplying locals. The one absolute rule, however, is that if there are enough old trained hands to do the cutting, no local shall be allowed to do pick-work, as his intelligence, knowledge, and honesty are not to be trusted without training.   The combination of piece pay for cutting and day pay for carrying is a happy one; as the piecework keeps the men moving, and they stir up the boys on day pay (Fig. 19).

In European countries this use of boys is scarcely possible owing to the national education.   In Greece as in England the boys are required to go to school, and their holidays there are not at a time suitable for excavating, while in England the holidays are occupied by the harvest.   Hence all work has to be done by men, at a higher rate of pay; and so

Figs. 19, 20. FILLING AND CARRYING, AT ABYDOS.

mechanical aids to moving earth would be more profitable than they are in Egypt.

It may be mentioned that the workers are always expected to provide their own picks and baskets in Egypt; while ropes, crowbars, and other tools only occasionally wanted are found by the master. If the daily tools were also provided, they would soon be spoiled, and need constant attention; it is bad enough to have to check and take care of ropes and special tools. The baskets brought up need to be looked at for size, especially those of local boys. When choosing boys, a fair size of basket should be insisted on as a condition of employment; and if small or broken baskets are brought up afterwards, the boy should be turned off, in order to bring a proper basket next day.

The two objects of excavations are (1) to obtain plans and topographical information, and (2) to obtain portable antiquities. For the purpose of securing antiquities it is Rewards. necessary to guard against the ignorance, the carelessness, and the dishonesty of the men employed. The best way to protect the interests of the work is to give rewards for all the things that are found, commonly called "the *bakhshish* system." If only half-a-dozen men are employed, and the master will take care to see that they never touch the work except while he is watching them, it may be practicable to do without *bakhshish*. But in the ordinary course of having one or two hundred men and boys at work over a large area, it is essential to pay partly by results, at least in the East; in Greece, owing to the large claims of the Government, this is scarcely practicable.

D

The actual amount given should be as much as a travelling dealer would pay to the peasant, were he buying the object. For small and very saleable things a high rate should be given ; for larger blocks, difficult to move, a lesser rate ; and for larger things of some hundredweights a nominal present may be given without any relation to the market value. On the whole the *bakhshish* is usually 5 to 10 per cent of the wages ; and as it is only about 1s. in the pound on the European values it is well worth while to secure better work by giving it. Moreover, it is not by any means overlooked in the estimate of the worth of the work, but—like the prizes of gold digging—it is more than discounted in the prospects which induce desirable men to come. The tenth of a chance of getting ten pounds is more attractive than the certainty of getting one pound in wages ; so the extra payments secure willing workers, even better than the same amount spread in regular pay.

It is by no means only as a safeguard to honesty. The observation of things, and the care required to avoid breakages, are two very necessary habits for good workmen. Many a small thing would be over-looked and lost if it were no benefit to the finder. And digging carefully so as to avoid breakages, makes a great difference to the returns obtained. When giving *bakhshish* on a broken thing, it is well to say how much more would have been given had it been perfect. And if fragments are missing, a large deduction should be made, and the balance promised if the pieces can be found. A fine flint knife, anciently broken, was produced with several chips missing ; I gave 4s. for it, but offered 16s.

more for the chips, which induced the men to sit down and turn over twenty tons of earth by hand, fingering every grain ; nearly every scrap was found, the men got the whole 20s., and I got the whole of the largest flint knife known. In another case I kept a lad sifting earth for three weeks, to find a minute head which he had lost. Nothing can ensure care better than paying for it ; while any bad carelessness or disobedience to orders is met by degrading a man to unprofitable work or dismissing him. The principle that the holder gets the *bakhshish* must even be extended to cases where one man has taken things from another man's hole ; the man who has lost the things is merely told that he should have taken better care of his work.

The account keeping is a serious matter, especially when the men are working far from home, as then they wish to be paid irregularly. There is first the account of earnings, by day or Accounts. by piecework ; second, the account of *bakhshish ;* third, the banking account of how much each man has due to him, or, if he has just drawn gold, perhaps a small balance against him ; and fourth, the advances for market and for drawing to send home. The simplest way of paying is Schliemann's, giving a day's pay to every man every night ; but it requires great quantities of change and a long time of delay to the workers and the master. Weekly payments are better, on the night before market day or on market morning. The account is read through to a man, his assent obtained to it ; he is asked if he wants to draw gold, and if not, the total is booked to him, added to his previous balance. Then for marketing, it is best to join the men in groups of six or eight together, and give the chief man of each group a sovereign to divide as they want it. After market he states how much each has had, and it is deducted from the balance of each man, while any unspent cash is returned.

Thus the amounts which should balance in weekly accounts are, for instance :—

RECEIVED.	£	PT.	SPENT.	£	PT.
Total to 17th Feb.	168	77	Total to 17th Feb.	182	34
on 19th ,,	10	...	Wages to 24th ,,	34	16
on 22nd ,,	5	...	Locals to 24th ,,	9	83
on 24th ,,	20	80	House	...	39
			Materials	...	64
Total received	204	59½	Personal drawings	5	...
Due to men	27	79			
Balancing total	232	41		232	41

This, of course, being the paymaster account, as apart from the accounts in chief, and from which the accounts in chief are made up by the head of a party.

It is necessary to take trouble to gain the confidence of the men ; they must be convinced of the master's good faith and precision. Whenever there is reasonable doubt on a point, they must always be given the benefit of it ; and plenty of patience is needed to hear their complaints, and to understand what is the real state of an objection. Some men are so puzzle-headed that they cannot remember their account clearly ; and if so, it is best to make them name some friend with whom all their accounts are settled. If any man wants to go far back in accounts—and sometimes they will raise a question

of four or five weeks before—then it is well to have
a friend as witness, who will see that it is right, and
close the matter, silencing any puzzled grumbling.
Egyptians will often dispute accounts against their
own interest, and remind the payer of amounts which
they have received that may have been overlooked.
But it is needful to show care and interest about the
smallest amounts, so as to maintain a sense of exact-
ness and precision with the men.

Some masters avoid going over accounts by giving
each man a card, and entering his account on it in
figures ; but as the man cannot check it without
asking a reader, this hardly meets the case.   Another
form of accounts is, however, understood and desired
by the men, in the form of a tally which every one
can check, and from which they can automatically
balance accounts at once.   A piece of sheet zinc is
ruled in columns (Fig. 21), each of 20 squares for
the 20 piastres in each dollar ; and every fifth column
is lined heavier, as marking a pound.   All amounts
earned are marked by spots in the columns, and
amounts paid are scored through.   Thus in this
example the earnings were 12, 2, 5, 9, 30, and 15
piastres ; the drawings were 17, 14, 11, 4, 2, $1\frac{1}{2}$, $6\frac{1}{2}$
piastres ; and the balance still due between the last
score and the last spot is 17 piastres, which any
man can count for himself.   Such a tally will hold
five pounds of accounts, or ten if ruled on both sides.

It hardly needs saying that a small amount of
doctoring is continually wanted.   Damages to hands
and limbs in moving heavy stones, bruises   Native ways.
and strains, sore eyes, malarial fever,
rheumatic headaches, indigestion, swellings and

gatherings, old sores, and many other small ailments are of daily occurrence. A stock of medicines, and some care in applying them, are necessary in any excavations. But it is necessary to refuse to give medicine to any one outside of the workmen : first,

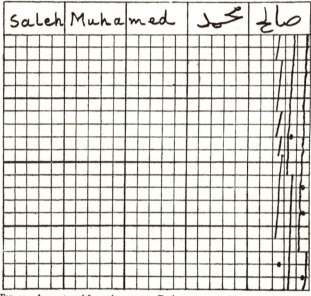

Fɪɢ. 21.—Account-card for native wages. Each square, one piastre. Each column, one dollar. A spot at each amount due. A line through the squares paid up.

because a gratis doctor would never have time to do other work ; second, on account of infection ; and third, because patients are an excuse for spies.

Having now noticed the men who are required, something may be said of those who are not required. The dealer and the spy are a constant plague. No man must be allowed to loaf about the work, or to

lie watching it from a look-out point. And any
troublesome men are best dealt with by taking shoes
or head-shawl from them, and offering to send the
clothes to the man's sheikh to be returned to him.
To get them he must give his name, and the name
of his sheikh ; and that no man will do, as he can
then be dropped on by the police in future. Not a
single loafer will ever give his name and sheikh, and
so they are well kept at bay by confiscating clothing
or tools. Once I took the donkey of a troublesome
man, who had fled from me ; and gave it up to his
sheikh, who came to intercede next day. Doubtless
it had to be redeemed by some blackmail to the
sheikh, and the needful lesson was taught. Dealers
are incessantly trying to get at the men, daily at
wells or as tobacco-sellers, and weekly in the market ;
and so any unexplained persons who are seen about
should be moved on and kept at a distance.

It is supposed by some that there is a solidarity
in the family of an Egyptian, which ensures that a
man's relatives know about his actions, and are
aware if he goes wrong. But various events have
shown that a man's own relatives may be quite in
the dark about his doings, and that a chance out-
sider may see, know, and tell things about a man
which are secret from his relatives living with him.
Hence the guarantee of a relative is worth practically
nothing, and every man must be taken on his own
merits. It must always be remembered that excavation is for the sake of archaeology, and is not
undertaken in the interest of the workman. Hence
any doubt about a man's character is sufficient reason
for not employing him. There is neither reason nor

use in making accusations, which after all it might
be impossible to prove.   But an unostentatious weeding out of men during the fluctuations of the work
is the best means of avoiding those who seem less
likely to be trustworthy.

A reason for not taking any man's recommendations is that the introduction to the work is sure to
be paid for ; and if Ibrahim begs you to employ
Aly, and succeeds, Aly will have to give him a lump
sum or a share of the wages.   Advice *for* a man
should therefore never be taken ; though advice
against a man may be disinterested and useful.

Fig. 22. Carrier boys throwing on mounds. Abydos.

Fig. 23. Town-site turned over, showing outer wall. Kahun.

CHAPTER IV

THE ARRANGEMENT OF WORK

A LARGE site, such as that of a temple or a town, may be attacked in several ways. The most cursory method is by trial pits in various spots ; Clearances. pits which, if they hit anything of importance, are likely to injure it, and certain to destroy its connection with other things. French explorers have a love for *faire quelques sondages*, a proceeding which often ruins a site for systematic work, and which never shows the meaning of the positions or the nature of the plan. If it is quite uncertain whether there be remains in the ground, the best examination is by parallel trenches, as such give a good view of the soil, while the stuff can be turned back and the trench filled behind if not wanted. In case of tracing a building, trenches cut along the lines of the walls are a good beginning ; and then if more is wanted, the plan is clear and the rooms can be emptied with foresight.

A favourite method with the older explorers was to clear out a whole area (Fig. 18) and throw the stuff all round the site. This may be needful in case of superimposed buildings, which must be

studied one by one, as only two or three periods
can be planned at once, and the upper have to be
removed before the lower can be cleared.   But such
a method is a clumsy waste in dealing with a simple
group of buildings.   The great difficulty of it is to
know where to place the stuff removed, so as not
to block future work.   Before beginning any large
excavation, the amount to be shifted should be
gauged, and the position of the stuff settled beforehand.   The great clearance on the side of the
Medum pyramid, to expose the temple, was planned
out with the position and size of each waste heap
in the mind's eye, and the system of paths by which
the stuff could be shifted with least fatigue.   It is
needful to continually adjust the moving, so as to
avoid lifting the stuff more than really needed ;
and any long run down of material, either towards
the digger or away from the thrower, should be
prevented, as it all has to be lifted again in some
shape.   Working at the foot of a long run of stuff
is entirely wrong ; such ground should be shifted in
successive levels, each level being discharged without
needing to raise the earth up again.   Excavations
at the Sphinx were carried on by the Government
with two men filling baskets with sand, which ran
down 20 feet from the surface to the bottom of a
pit ; and the baskets were then carried up by a
long train of children very slowly climbing up out
of the pit on a sand slope at the angle of running
sand.   Thus nearly the whole labour was wasted by
not filling the baskets at the surface and carrying
them directly away.   Whenever a large pit is needed
it should be begun of full size, and lowered equally

Fig. 24. CUTTING DOWN FROM THE TOP EDGE OF THE WORK.

CEMETERY WORK

Fig. 25. Mounds, at Yehudiyeh. | Fig. 26. Sarcophagi, Abydos.

all over, so that nothing runs down during the work.

For moving earth to a distance there is no way so simple and adaptable as a line of carrier boys (Fig. 22). Over flat ground this is the best way up to distances of 50 or 100 yards; for longer discharges it may be better to lay down a light railway and use trucks. The line of boys is the only practicable way if the stuff has to be carried up a slope to discharge, or taken over irregular paths out of the work, as is often the case. The railway needs much time for rearranging different points of collection and discharge; and must be in duplicate, or else the work will be at a stand-still during re-arrangement. A boy will carry 20 to 30 lbs. in a load, about 20 journeys an hour for 100 yards discharge, thus moving about 2 tons a day. So the cost is about a piastre a cubic metre for shifting 100 yards.

But far the more economical and rapid work is that of turning over whenever practicable. If a site has not been often rebuilt upon, the way is to start by a long clearance at one edge; and then a line of men steadily cut from one side of the trench and throw back on the other (Fig. 24), so that the trench moves across the whole site, and every pound of earth is turned over. Each man needs a frontage of between 4 and 6 metres in width; and the trench, if open along, should have a clear bottom of at least 2 metres, from back to front of the work. More usually it is worked in compartments, each man clearing about 4 metres square, and throwing into his previous

Turning over.

hole ; each hole is then gauged when empty and the pay assessed.   If a town is cleared (Fig. 23), then it is done chamber by chamber, each being emptied over the wall into the previous chamber. The corners of the chambers can just be left visible for making a plan afterwards.   A great advantage of this way is that the ground is finally left covered, so there is no great waste heap, and the walls are all covered over again to save them from future destruction.

Where a deep hollow has to be cleared out it is a wasteful plan to let the boys walk out with the **Raising earth.** basket of earth, as they have to raise the body, which is about four times the weight of their load.   So soon as the rise is as steep as one in four, it is best to form a fixed chain of boys (Fig. 27), each standing in a permanent place, and handing the baskets up from one to another.   About 5 feet apart horizontally is as far as is useful ; or in case of steep work (as out of pits) the vertical lift may be 3 or 4 feet (Fig. 1).   A sufficient number of collectors at the bottom and throwers at the top are of course needed to keep the chain in full work (Fig. 28).   A well-proportioned gang should not have any accumulations along it, and must be quietly watched from time to time to see that all parts work equally.   If the baskets of earth lag at any point and accumulate, the boys before the point must be thinned, and those beyond it increased.   A favourite plan of the boys is to let a basket lie un-shifted and then stand upon it, as a full basket of earth gives a pleasant footing, and there is one less to keep moving.   In this way most of the baskets

CHAINS OF WORKERS.

Fig. 27. At tomb of Usertesen II. | Fig. 28. At tomb of King Den.

can be quietly suppressed, and yet every one remains as busy as they can be with the short stock of baskets that remain. All such misuse of baskets must be stopped at once; but old burst baskets may be used thus with advantage.

This system of lifting is also used in a surprising way for vertical tomb pits. An Egyptian man will stand all day with his feet on opposite sides of a pit in foot-holes, and stoop down to take a full basket from a man below at the level of his feet; then raise himself, and lift the basket up at arms' length above his head, thus lifting it 6 or 7 feet. Three men will thus empty out a pit to 20 feet deep; but such men are usually old tomb-robbers, and must be employed with circumspection. More usually ropes are used, one tied to each handle of a basket, and pulled up by a pair of men. The earth is best left in the carrying basket, which is laid in the roped basket at the bottom, and taken out of it at the surface. If the pit is rotten and wide at the top, the basket has to be swung across the top two or three times, until on letting the ropes loose it flies out 10 or 20 feet to the side of the pit, where it is caught by the emptying boy. Clever rope-men will let a basket fly so as to catch on the top of the dump heap and turn over, so that it only needs clearing loose to let it go back again. The ropes need careful watching; the men love to tie knots in them, to grip by, whereby they wear through at the knots and drop to pieces; also the ropes are dragged on the edge of the pit, so as to serve as a friction-clutch when changing hands, thus wearing the rope out in two days instead of two months; the sides of the pit should be looked at to see if there is any sawing by the rope, and if so, the men must be stopped. They also cut off pieces if the ropes are long ; and it is best to have all ropes in standard lengths of 8 metres, these when doubled thrice over down to 1 metre length are quickly tested for length, and then hanked in the middle to put by. Lastly, if not regularly delivered into store every night, the ropes are not returned when a pit is finished ; and then they vanish, and a fresh pair is asked for when the next pit goes deep.

Another favourite misuse of ropes is to lash them round blocks of stone which have to be dragged, and thus cut the rope into scraps by wearing on the ground. Ropes can generally be put round the sides of a stone, and kept in place by some old scraps passing beneath.

One of the most careful kinds of work, to which only good men can be trained, is that of tracing out
Tracing walls. unbaked brick walls buried in rubbish. The surrounding earth is derived from the crumbling and washing down of the earthen wall, and therefore it is indistinguishable from the average of the bricks themselves. Hence, if the bricks are uniform in colour, and the mud mortar is like them, the building and its débris are all alike. The best way to examine brickwork is by scraping a face of the wall, and then peeling it quite clean with a dinner-knife ; such a clean smooth surface seen in shadow will show whatever can possibly be made out of the differences of colour and texture. Vertical joints are worth far more than horizontal, as often fallen bricks may lie as if built together. If possible the joints should be observed by differences of colour,

and the bricks measured for comparison with others ;
as the sizes vary from 7 inches to 2 feet in length,
and but seldom range over half an inch in any one
building period, the size will go a long way in showing a connection of age.   If the bricks cannot be
distinguished even after leaving the face to dry for
some days, the earth should be searched by peck-
ing with a trowel or knife to see if there is dirt
in it : only in late times are pottery chips found
usually in bricks, and charcoal scraps are very rare,
hence pottery and charcoal almost prove the earth to
be mere wash and rubbish.   The clearing back of
dirty earth to a vertical face of clean clay is a satisfactory evidence of a wall.   But sometimes the filling
is so clean that there is no difference between it and
the wall.   Then the relative hardness will often serve
to distinguish one from the other ; and this is a main
means of discrimination by the workmen, who will
often tell a wall entirely by the touch under the pick.
Failing all these tests, and the strata of dirt beds,
the film of stucco on the wall face will sometimes
show up, but may leave a doubt as to which side is
the wall.   In the last resource the stuff should be
searched with a magnifier to see the hollows left by
decomposed straw dust : in kneaded brick these
hollows lie in every direction ; in blown dust and
wash they lie nearly all horizontal.   It is often needful to spend half-an-hour testing and tracing out the
line of a wall, fixing the face and the top and base
of it ; and such work may give the only evidence of
a temple or important building.

CHAPTER V

RECORDING IN THE FIELD

AFTER finding things the first consideration is to record and preserve all the information about them.

Need of record.

The most ignorant dealer or plunderer may be a very successful digger, but he will not care for the value of a record. Recording is the absolute dividing line between plundering and scientific work, between a dealer and a scholar. The most blue-blooded *dilettante* collector who digs to possess fine things, but records no facts about them, is below the level of the dealer who will publish an illustrated priced catalogue, and state what was found together, and the details of the discovery. The unpardonable crime in archaeology is destroying evidence which can never be recovered ; and every discovery does destroy evidence unless it is intelligently recorded. Our museums are ghastly charnel-houses of murdered evidence ; the dry bones of objects are there, bare of all the facts of grouping, locality, and dating which would give them historical life and value. And it is only the self-evident facts of age that we already know, which can be observed in such a useless condition. So ignorant are

48

curators that they will even divide up a tomb-group
of objects, which are the keys to knowledge, and
foolishly scatter them up and down the galleries
merely as second-rate specimens of what is already
there, without any date or history. This is actually
the case in the three largest national museums. It
is therefore imperative not only to record, but also
to publish, the facts observed ; so that when in
future the elements of scientific management may
come to be understood, a fit curator may succeed in
reuniting the long-severed information, as is being
to some extent happily done at Dublin.

In recording, the first difficulty is to know what
to record. To state every fact about everything
found would be useless, as no one could wade
through the mass of statements. It would be like a
detective who would photograph and measure every
man on London Bridge to search for a criminal : the
complication would entirely defeat the object. It is
absolutely necessary to know how much is already
known before setting about recording more. In
some periods, such as the XVIIIth Dynasty, so much
is ascertained that it is seldom that new facts can be
brought to light ; and only fine or unusual discoveries
are worth full publication. On the other hand, in
such an age as the early dynasties our only resource
lies in complete records of the levels or collocations
of hundreds of pots, whole or broken ; and most
important historical conclusions may hang on a
single potsherd.

It is plain therefore that the accuracy and certainty
of the record is necessary. At the moment that a
fact is before the eye,—a fact which may never

E

be seen again, and perhaps never paralleled,—it is

Value of record.   needful for the observer to make certain
of all the details, to verify every point
which is of fresh value, and to record all that is new
with certainty and exactitude.   Statements with a
query, or a doubt about them, are worth nothing in
themselves, and can only serve to add to the range
of similar facts that may be safely recorded from
elsewhere.   Everything seen should be mentally
grasped, and its meaning and bearings comprehended
at the moment of discovery, so clearly that a
definitive statement can be made, which shall be as
certain and as absolute as anything can be which
depends on human senses.   The observer should at
least feel no possible doubts or qualms about his
recorded facts ; and what uncertainties there are
should only be those which lie beyond his percep-
tions.   It is well to work slowly over all the petty
details of an important discovery, perhaps for half
an hour, while considering all the facts and their
meaning, before finally and irrevocably removing the
main evidences of position.   All this needs practice,
and a full knowledge of what is important and what
is trivial.

And not only should such a record be made at
the time, but the record should be presented finally

Resulting view.   in an intelligible form.   To empty the
contents of note-books on a reader's
head is not publishing.   A mass of statements which
have no point, and do not appear to lead to any
conclusion or generalisation, cannot be regarded as
an efficient publication.   The meaning of each fact
should be made apparent, and the relative importance

of the details should be kept in view, so as to present the conclusions as a picture, in which each touch is in its proper place, and where each point adds to the whole without being disproportionately treated. Thus the final result is a statement much like what might have been written by a contemporary of the times in question ; proved and enforced at each point by the various facts discovered.

In many cases our materials are not enough to give such a picture; and then, either the blanks must be noted and the limits of uncertainty stated, or else, at the worst, the facts must be grouped, and their results stated, leaving the question with two or more solutions open to future settlement.

Thus the final result to be aimed at is a picture full of detail and accuracy ; and, where material is insufficient, with the limits of doubt clearly laid down, so that fresh material can at once be incorporated, and its value seen and grasped, so soon as it may be discovered.

A very needful part of the recording is the marking of the objects with their source. Generally each part of a site is distinguished by a letter, and each group of objects found *Marking.* in that part by a number ; thus a cemetery may be E, another adjoining it on different ground F, yet another G, a temple site T, and so on, sometimes using up the whole alphabet on a varied district. Then E 17, F 8, G 65, will be different tombs in those cemeteries, as denoted in the note-book and on the objects. Every bone of a skeleton should be marked, and always on one fixed position for each bone. It is best to trust to writing the reference

with China ink on the base or back of most objects;
for pottery and coarse things Brunswick black
thinned with turpentine is best; for dark stones
scratching the number is safest, and also for wet
pottery at the time it is found.   Jewellers' tag-labels
with strings are useful for small objects.   It is very
unsafe to trust labelling only to the wrapping papers,
which may be all thrown away; separate labels
should be wrapped with the things if they cannot be
marked otherwise.

The nature of the notes must vary with each
kind of material and each period; but we may here
Nature of notes.   give some examples of the nature of
such records.

Town Plan.—Survey of every wall of each
house; thickness of each wall (easily neglected);
reveals of doorways; doorsills if of stone; sizes of
bricks; levels of top and base of each wall if any
rebuilt or superimposed; contents of each chamber,
note if on floor or in filling; objects buried in floors;
special note of position of exactly dated objects;
copies of any frescoes or decoration.

Tomb.—Position relative to other tombs.   Size of
pit, direction, depth.   Position of chamber.   Filling
intact, or estimate of time that it has stood open
anciently by the weathering of the sides.   Objects
found loose in filling.   Chamber plan.   Primary or
secondary burial.   Position of body, head direction,
face direction, attitude of body and limbs.   Position
of beads and small objects on body.   Note if beads
follow any pattern or order; record order of as long
groups of beads as possible for rethreading; wrappings,
amount and nature.   Coffin or cartonnage; inscrip-

tion and figures, if any, often need copying or photographing before removal, as they may fall to pieces.
Skull and jaw to be removed for measurement ; or,
if in rarer periods, whole skeleton to be preserved.
Position and nature of all offerings and objects
placed in the tomb. Copies of any inscriptions or
paintings on the walls of the tomb.

To such outlines of the usual character of records
are added any special details which are but rarely
found ; but the above will serve to remind an excavator of what must always be looked for.

In making a plan of any large area, such as a
town, it is best to start with a rough key-plan divided
into a few dozen squares, each row of
squares lettered, each column of squares   Planning.
numbered, so that every square is designated, as
B 5, etc. (Fig. 32). Then the detailed plan of each
square is to be made on one opening of a note-book
of squared paper, the openings running A 1, A 2,
A 3 ; B 1, B 2, B 3, etc. Thus any connection from
one page to another can be found at once by looking
for the next letter or number : the whole plan is
in the pocket, and can be added to, chamber by
chamber, as the clearing progresses. It need hardly
be said that every plan or detail should be
drawn north upwards in the note-book. Main lines
are of course to be connected together by long lines
of measurement.

As a general principle it is best to measure
positions of as many points as possible along one
single line of measurement, rather than take many
piece-meal short distances and add them together,
Thus (Fig. 29) a series of walls should be stated as,

66, 76, 201, 220, 257, 269, 330, 353, 434, 446 inches, rather than as lengths of 66, 10, 25, 19, 37, 12, 61, 23, 81, and 12 inches; for the total is more accurate when measured all in one, the positions are plotted quicker, and the comparison with any symmetric lengths of the building are easier made on the spot, so as to detect errors.

In the direct measurement of groups of walls, etc.,

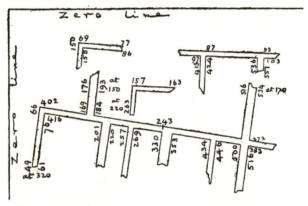

Fig. 29.—Example of a plan measured entirely from two bounding lines.

it is the quicker and more accurate method to adopt two outside sighting lines, say one along the north, the other along the east, of the ground, marked out by high walls or large stones always visible, and then measure every point out to the two sighting lines at right angles.   Spaces of over 100 feet across can be divided into separate groups.

The general use of instruments cannot be entered upon here.   But amongst the means of work the divided rod is indispensable, and it is all that is wanted for most small buildings that are met with. The tape is the most practical for distances of 10 to 50 feet ; and the steel tape for accurate measuring of base lines, or long distances. The box-sextant is for very broken ground, and isolated details, or if working alone ; and the theodolite for accurate work anywhere between the accuracy of, say, 1 inch on 500 feet and the refinement of a $\frac{1}{4}$ of an inch on a mile. The plane table may be convenient for approximate plans, and is simple and rapid to use. The prismatic compass is of use for the directions of single blocks or fragments of wall, and is handy for rough topography (generally with paced distances), or for underground passages.

In considering the accuracy required, if dimensions in figures are to be given, then minute measurement is wanted, somewhat more accurate than the original workmanship. But where only a plan is to be produced, it is seldom practicable to show more accuracy than $\frac{1}{100}$th inch on a book page 10 inches high, or $\frac{1}{1000}$th of the whole, and therefore it is of no use to measure closer than 1 inch on a space of 200 feet or so across.

It need hardly be said that the barbarous irregular fractions, such as $\frac{3}{8}$ of an inch to a foot or to a mile, should never be used for plotting. Plotting. Simple decimal scales should alone be used, and generally $\frac{1}{100}$th is the most suitable and easy for all plans of ordinary buildings, towns, etc. ; this is further reduced by photolithography to whatever scale will best fit the size of publication.

Though the ordinary methods of survey need not be stated here, the box-sextant is so seldom seen that

some account should be given of its use. The
objection to its use on short distances, that parallax
between the direct and reflected ray causes errors,
can be avoided by overlapping the images about $\frac{3}{4}$
inch, the usual amount of the parallax. The main
use of the sextant is for three-point survey. Over
broken ground where many isolated points have to

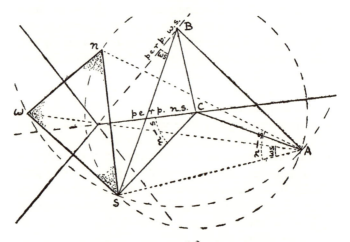

Fig. 30.—Method of plotting a three-point survey, *n, w, s,* the three fixed points.
A the point to be found. B, C, centres of struck circles.

be fixed, within a few inches on a few hundred feet,
there is no method so quick and useful as the nautical
three-point method, when improved by rigid plotting.
At any three points which shall be visible from the
whole of the ground, and within its general plane,
three signals are placed, best lettered by the quarter
of the horizon nearest to each, say *n, s, w.* The three
points must be so placed that the one circle passing
through them all shall not pass through points

needed in the survey ; otherwise they may be in any position, though best as a triangle of about equal sides. The three angles and one side are to be measured, thus defining the whole triangle. Then at any point to be fixed, A, the two angles between n to s and w to s are measured with the sextant, and these suffice to fix the position. For plotting (Fig. 30), lay down the triangle of the three fixed points, say to scale $\frac{1}{100}$th (the triangle with shaded corners n, s, w), and the perpendiculars to each side of it ; this is most accurately done by a large protractor with vernier, setting out the radii and perpendiculars of the triangle from its centre. Then tabulate the half of each base × cotan. angles observed on that base, *e.g.*

		logs.	n.n.	logs.	n.n.	logs.	n.n.	
½ bases	n	·27314		s ·36621		w ·29223		n
× cotan.	1	·43223	2·705	·26272	1·831	...	...	
angles at	2	·56671	3·687	...	...	·48214	3·035	
places 1, 2, 3	3	·41995	2·630	...	...	·67709	4·754	

Here the log. half base n to s is ·27314 ; this added to log. cotan. of angle subtended by $n - s$ from station 1 is log. ·43223, giving a value 2·705 inches. From station 1 the angle $s - w$ was observed ; and from stations 2 and 3 the angle $w - n$ was observed. All this calculation can be rapidly done in this form, placing the sheet upon the log. book, with the written log. half base next below the printed log. cotan. angle, and writing down the sum of the two against the number of the station. Then on the plan, plot these (½ base × cotan.) on the perpendiculars of their respective bases as at B and C, marking the station number to each. Then with compasses sweep an arc from one centre B, with radius B*s* equal to the distance from the centre to its two points of the triangle. The same from the other centre C that has the same number of station. The intersection of the arcs is the point A of that station on the plan.

Of course the prolonged perpendiculars (broken lines) are used as often as the direct perpendiculars; the *aspect* of the angle from the station, whether $n - s$ or $s - n$ showing on which half of the perpendicular we should lay off the centre. For angles over 90° the complement of the angle should be used in calculation, the centre then laid off on the wrong half of the perpendicular, and the arc swept across the right half. This mode of plotting gives the fullest accuracy, such as is never possible with the use of station-pointers, or trial and error devices which are used in nautical survey. A field of 40 stations can be easily calculated in an hour, and plotted in a couple of hours more. If it is needful to work any point with pure calculation instead of plotting, it can be accurately done by the principle that the line joining the two centres of arcs, B and C, forms with their common point *s* an equal and opposite triangle to that which they form with the survey point A. It will be seen on looking at the diagram that $w - s$, the angle by which B is plotted, is equal to the angle $w - s$ from A; and similarly the angle of the half base $n - s$ from C, is equal to $n - s$ from A. Hence the points *n*, *s*, *w* subtend from A, the observed angles, and A is the point from which they must have been observed.

For levelling, the handiest instrument is a short rigid pendulum, with mirror attached, to hang truly vertical. The reflection of the eye back to itself is then a truly horizontal line, and can be sighted on to any distance. The pendulum is best made about 5 inches long, with tetrahedral net of suspension thread, to avoid twisting, passing through two eyes on the mirror and two eyes on the holder, and a covering tube to shield it from wind. With this, readings can easily be taken to an inch on 100 feet, and this is sufficient accuracy for most archaeological work.

CHAPTER VI

COPYING

A very needful branch of recording is the taking impressions of inscriptions and flat reliefs. The usual method is by wet squeezing of **Paper squeezes.** paper, which may be made up of any thickness, from a true mould to a slight surface impression. If a mould is wanted for future casting, a tough rag paper without much size should be used ; but good newspaper will do. The tougher the paper is when wet, the better. The stone must be thoroughly cleaned and soaked. The paper is cut to the size, and, if less than the stone, in two or more sheets. A sheet is then put in a basin of water, rolled about to soak, and then gathered into a ball and rolled between the hands to break the grain, just short of pulping the surface ; next shaken out like a wet handkerchief, and then laid on the stone with enough slack to go into all the hollows. It is then gently beaten with a spoke-brush until it is pushed into the hollows (Fig. 33). If they are deep it is needful to use strips of paper soaked and pulped, and laid by finger in the hollows, so as to nearly fill them. Finally, a severe beating is given to the whole, as violent as can be done without tearing the paper. The paper should be pulped on the stone, and driven into every crack and porosity ; using a second, and even a third, sheet to bind it together. The pulp in the hollows should be kneaded in with the sharp edge of the brush-back, using the whole weight of the body to force it home. About 50 square feet of such work is as much as can be done in a day. The precautions are : avoid bubbles of water or air below the paper, beat quite straight without dragging, and see that there is no creeping of the paper or shifting on the stone. When quite dry and hard the cast may be carefully peeled off. After heating and waxing, plaster casts may be taken from it, with a slight oiling between each using.

A slighter working is enough on shallow inscriptions ; but such squeezes generally need to be taken off while wet, and allowed to dry alone, or else the paper drags flat out of the hollows when contracting in drying. This is specially the case on polished granite, where there is no grip on the surface.

Surface impressions of incised carving may be taken with a single sheet of paper beaten just enough to catch the edges of the cutting ; and such make excellent bases for inking over to produce a facsimile drawing (Fig. 31). The impression is so much better on the inner side, that the inking is done on that, and the figures are thus reversed in the plate.

But on all coloured work, and many kinds of tender stones, wet squeezing is a crime, as it destroys the original. Fatuous tourists **Dry squeezes.** and brazen students have wrecked innumerable monuments by wet squeezing, and it is now necessarily prohibited in Egypt unless special permission is obtained to do some object which cannot be injured by it. Another system, that of dry squeezing, I therefore introduced when doing the Medum tombs. A sheet of thin paper is held

Fig. 31.—Copy made by inking a paper squeeze, 1 :8. A part of the Israel stele, with the name Israel in the last line but one.

over the stone, and it is pressed over each edge of the cutting so as to leave a bend in the surface. Then, laid on a drawing-board, with an oblique lighting, the bends are all drawn on with pencil, checking by comparison with the stone. Sometimes it is best to draw by lamplight, and check with the stone afterwards. The drawing should always begin at the bottom right hand, so as not to press out the impression by the hand ; and the sheets must not be rolled before being pencilled. For small lines, a piece of indiarubber should be used to press the paper into the hollows. For the outlines of reliefs the thumb nail must be used. This system is quicker and more accurate than any reduced-scale hand drawing. Over large wall surfaces the sheets should be placed in regular rows, lettered A, B, C

A 1	A 2	A 3	A 4	A 5	A 6	A 7	A 8
B 1	B 2	B 3	B 4	B 5	B 6	B 7	B 8
C 1	C 2	C 3	C 4	C 5	C 6	C 7	C 8
D 1	D 2	D 3	D 4	D 5	D 6	D 7	D 8
E 1	E 2	E 3	E 4	E 5	E 6	E 7	E 8
F 1	F 2	F 3	F 4	F 5	F 6	F 7	F 8

FIG. 32.—System of numbering sheets of connected drawings.

(Fig. 32), and each sheet numbered in the row, so that A 3, B 3, C 3, come one below the other. The register of positions is kept by marking a minute cross with pencil on the wall, so that the corners of four sheets will fall between the four arms of the cross. Thus each fresh sheet is placed exactly to fit the sheets which have preceded it, in the row and in the column. Any large blanks or injuries should have their corresponding sheets duly lettered (even if nothing is on them), and put with the drawings, so that there shall be no hitch in placing them all in one great sheet afterwards.

It may be convenient to join up the sheets, and then redivide the drawings at suitable spaces between the subjects for convenience of packing. To join the sheets they must be laid together in position, a slight cut then made with a knife to mark two sheets across the joint; then turned back-up, adjusted by the cut, and a strip of adhesive paper put on the joint, dabbed down and not rubbed along. Thus large sculptured walls can be copied sheet by sheet, joined up, inked in, and then photo-lithographed for plates. It is needful to remember that the Postal Union will take rolls up to 60 centimetres length and 21 cm. diameter, as ordinary parcels up to 5 kilograms; or 75 cm. length if not over 10 cm. diameter and 2 kilograms of weight, by book post, open at ends.

Beside the direct material for publishing in plates, it is often desirable to take casts and impressions, both for future reference and also as a step toward a photograph (Fig. 34).

Casting.

The making of paper impressions or squeezes has already been noted. Casting with plaster of Paris is the principal mode of reproduction, and is such a detailed business in itself that only a few notes can be given here, such as might possibly be wanted in field work. The fine work for museum purposes is outside of our aim here. The main point in handling wet plaster is rapidity; and for that everything must be ready, and the exact plan of work and amount of plaster settled beforehand. A basin should be used with water equal to about two-thirds of the volume of plaster required. Into this shake or sift dry plaster rapidly, until the water is just filled up with

CASTING.

| Fig. 33. Paper squeeze. XII Dyn. Goddess Nekheb. | Fig. 34. Plaster cast from paper. Philistine. XX Dyn. |

it, and no free water left on the top ; it is then well proportioned, and should be violently stirred with a large flat spoon or slip of wood and poured out in an even stream, beginning with the middle if a flat mould, and flattening it out to the edges. It is best to have rather too little than too much; as a fresh lot can be mixed, with the hardened pieces of the first lot, to serve for a backing ; the first lot being, of course, spread over the whole face to begin with. Strings, or strips of butter-muslin, should be put through the mass, if it is large, so as to prevent it falling to pieces if broken later on. Excellent casts are made with a thin skin of plaster on a backing of muslin put on a frame ; but this requires more skill than plain work. About 10 minutes after casting the back should be scraped down level, or planed with a wide-mouthed hand plane, which is a very useful tool in finishing casts. No cast of any large size should be left without even support for some hours after casting, as it will settle out of shape if strained. Small quantities of plaster are best mixed with a pocket knife in the palm of the hand.

Moulds for casting are usually of clay for a large scale, but that is not likely to be used in the field-work. The division of the clay is best done by bedding threads along the face of the object at the lines required, and then pulling them up to cut the clay. The face of the object requires French chalk (steatite powder) on it to prevent cohesion ; oiling or greasing spoils the face of the original. For field-work paper moulds are best, and the preparation of these as wet squeezes has been already described. To fit the squeeze for use as a mould, it should be

F

heated and brushed with melted beeswax on the face, without necessarily soaking it through. Any places that are shiny when cold should be warmed and rubbed with cotton wool, so that the face is the true paper cast. Then slightly oil between each plaster casting, or else the warmth of the setting plaster will make the wax stick to it. Several casts can be taken from one paper, if it is carefully handled in peeling it from the plaster each time. Paper impressions of cylinders are best made with blotting-paper, unrolled wet, and left to dry. To remove the cockling of drying, spread a thin coat of stiff paste on card, and press the paper squeeze lightly on it.

Guttapercha moulds are best if many copies are required. To get a sharp impression in this tough material a preliminary mould should be made, of the right shape, but not sharp on the face. This should be thoroughly cooled in water for an hour or more, and then a small quantity of guttapercha from boiling water should be laid in the hard mould and the object pressed in very rapidly and with maximum pressure. Thus the hot material is forced firmly against every part and takes a brilliant impression. Such moulds are used for electrotyping as well as for plaster work. To produce a smooth face to a lump of hot guttapercha, it should be pulled outwards from the middle to all sides by thumbs and fingers, so as to produce a fresh torn face over the whole upper surface.

Sealing-wax is one of the handiest materials, and is used professionally for all the coin reproductions that are published. Only the best wax is of any use for impressions. It should never be allowed to burn or blaze, nor even to boil, but should be gently heated until a large mass will fall quite readily. The object should be wetted moderately just before impressing. So soon as the wax is tough the object should be lifted slightly to make certain that it has not stuck, and then pressed down again till cold. If it has stuck it must be pulled away at once, and the wax picked off while tough. Sealing-wax casts must be oiled before plaster is put to them ; and oil does not soften or deteriorate sealing-wax if left on for years. Beeswax, or, better, the mixture called " dentist's wax," makes good impressions, and may be used for moulds.

Tin-foil is most useful for rapid impressions, especially from a fragile or delicate object. The thinnest should be used, such as is wrapped round chocolate. To preserve the form of tin-foil it may be squeezed into place with a back of beeswax, and so form a facing to a wax mould for casting a plaster positive. Or it may be pressed alone (forcing it on with soft indiarubber or cotton wool), and then floated, back up, on water, while blazing sealing-wax is dropped into it to form a backing. This mode is very handy for coin impressions, which will travel safely in this form and look well. For round objects, such as cylinders, a tin-foil impression should be made, beating the foil in with a soft tooth-brush ; then the foil is to be uncoiled, by rolling it upon wax so that the curve is removed without flattening the impression ; it is then ready for a plaster casting, giving a flat cast of the round cylinder. In all cases thin gold-foil would be far better than tin-foil ; and such an impression might even be preferred to the original object by some Oriental officials.

Drawing is still the main resource for illustration, although photographic processes occupy so important a place. Hand-work is essential for plans, it is the more useful method for inscriptions, and it is the more convenient method for most small objects. There is generally some interpretation needed, to show details which could not possibly all be visible in one uniform lighting, as in a photograph ; and this can only be done by drawing all that can be seen in varying lights and aspects. Another superiority of outline drawings is that they are far more easily looked over and referred to than a much less distinct photograph. And lastly, they cost a third or a quarter of the amount for publication. The proper scope of photographs is stated in the next section.

Drawing.

As drawing is almost always to be reproduced by photolithography, or by zinc block, it is essential to have it entirely in full black and white without any grey or half tones. Hence the contrast should be kept as strong as possible ; and only China ink of full blackness should be used for fine lines. In wide, coarse work, as full-sized inscriptions from walls, a common writing-ink evaporated to denser quality may be used. Ebony stain, which some use, has the disadvantage of spreading badly if it chances to be wetted. A smooth, glazy-faced paper is good for fine lines, and does not rag up under the pen. Cardboard is pleasant to use, but is awkward to send by post ; whereas paper drawings roll up safely in a tube.

A cardinal rule in drawing is that the finest line should come out to $\frac{1}{300}$ inch when the subject is reduced to the plate size. Thus a drawing to be reduced to $\frac{1}{3}$ by photolithography should have its finest lines $\frac{1}{100}$ inch thick. This line of $\frac{1}{300}$ inch is the finest which is safe not to break up in reproducing; and of course it spreads a little in the printing. For very slight shade lines rather thinner lines may be used, as it is no disadvantage if they should break.

It is very desirable to have similar objects all reduced to the same scale. For pottery $\frac{1}{6}$ is a convenient reduction; for stones vases $\frac{1}{3}$; for metal tools and small objects $\frac{1}{2}$. The drawings of pottery and stone vases are easiest to do on scales $\frac{1}{4}$ and $\frac{1}{2}$, as the measured diameters have to be laid off as radii from the axis, needing halving throughout. The further reduction is done when photographing for the lithographs; and it is always best to have such a reduction to $\frac{2}{3}$, if not to $\frac{1}{2}$, of the size of the drawing, in order to make it come out more delicate than the hand-work. A very useful system for recording groups of small objects, especially such as are found together, is to lay them out on a sheet (say double the plate size), as arranged for the plate, and then run a pencil round the outlines, and add as much detail as may be needful to explain the objects; thus a pictorial inventory is made quickly, and is far more useful and easier for reference than any written inventory (Fig. 35). The pencil should have the wood split off one side of the lead, and be sharpened by cutting to a chisel-edge on the opposite side. Thus the point is vertically under the guiding side; and when held carefully upright, outlines can well be run from surfaces half an inch or even an inch above the paper. The size of the sheet will, of course, depend on the amount of reduction intended. For numbering the figures printed numbers can be gummed on to the drawing.

For vases, block tints are more satisfactory than

FIG. 35.—Part of an inventory sheet, recording pieces of ivory carving, 1 : 3.

outlines. So the drawing can be filled up with a wash of ink. Or if section lines are wanted it is best to draw the section line, and block out the ground outside of the vase, leaving the vase white on a black ground ; then have this reversed, black for white, in the photolithographing. The vases may be printed in any colour which is suitable.

The method for drawing a completed form of a

Fig. 36. Frame for drawing
fragments of vases.

Fig. 37. Weathered grave-stone ;
unsanded, and sanded.

vase from fragments is to place the brim and the base (the curves of which can be accur-

ately measured against a series of concentric circles) into their true positions, to a vertical axis ; and then, if there is no complete connection, to adjust their height on their axis so that their curvatures (including other pieces which join them) fall into one line. It is easier to do this with the mouth downwards. A frame is made (Fig. 36), with a vertical rod sliding up and down over the middle ; a card with concentric circles on it is placed on the floor of the frame, and centred under the rod. Taking a piece of a brim, it is rocked to and fro until it touches the card all along the edge, and a leg of wax is stuck on so as to keep it at that angle. It is then slid about till the curve fits between the concentric circles. A piece of base has its curvature measured, by fitting a sheet of celluloid ruled with concentric circles to the curve of it. It is then fixed on the lower end of the vertical rod with some wax, so that the rod is in its axis. Then the rod is slid down in its grooves until the curves of the piece of base and of the piece of brim fall into one line. For drawing the form the radius of the brim and of the base are already measured ; the height is taken as it stands in the frame, also the greatest radius at the shoulder, the angle of the side with the base, and sometimes the height from the brim to the curve at several different radii, read off by sliding a graduated square on the concentric circles to touch the curve. After plotting all these dimensions the curve is drawn in by freehand, looking carefully at the fragments in position.

For hand copying inscriptions of a small size, a good method is to fold over the paper at each line that is done, and draw the signs one by one on to the fresh edge of paper held side by side on the stone ; thus there is no strain or loss of time by looking to and fro and finding the place, no chance of omissions, and the facsimile is as accurate as possible. This is especially for copying ink writing and graffiti. When making a reduced copy by hand it is best to have a sheet of card under the paper ruled in squares (of $\frac{1}{4}$ or up to 2 inches), with thick lines. These show through the paper, and a frame of strings or threads is put over the stone, of a larger size, agreeing to the scale of reduction intended ; *e.g.* for reducing a wall to $\frac{1}{5}$, have card ruled in 1 inch squares, and a frame of strings 5 inches apart over the wall. For lines or columns of inscription it does to rule the column lines and only have a long scale on a strip of wood put alongside of the column which is being copied, so as to tally with the lines seen through the paper.

Copying inscriptions.

CHAPTER VII

PHOTOGRAPHING

PHOTOGRAPHS are essential for all objects of artistic interest, and for expressing rounded forms for which elaborate shading would otherwise be needed. Views of the excavations and buildings are also wanted. And it is desirable to publish photographs as well as drawings of very important carvings, in order to guarantee the accuracy of the drawing, which is the more useful edition for most purposes.

Though the ordinary knowledge of photography must be taken for granted here, there are many details and preferences which are special to this kind of work. The bane of practical photography is the rich amateur, who insists on useless luxury of apparatus, and has set a fashion in fittings which is absurdly complex. It is undesirable to have a specially compact camera, as steadiness and convenience in use are sacrificed for lightness and slightness, which are no object in a fixed camp. An old-fashioned bulky camera is better for stationary work. I have long used a tin-plate camera with plain draw-body in two pieces; the benefit when

Camera.

enlarged photographs are needed is found by taking it apart, and inserting a card tube, made up when wanted to any length required for the enlargement. Some very simple, adaptable camera is best, with a large plate-magazine attached to it, so that some dozens can be carried at once. For ordinary views and small-scale objects a simple hand camera is best. A pattern should be adopted which may be the least liable to get out of order in a very dusty and gritty climate ; of the simplest mechanism, with a plain thrown-down pattern, to carry a dozen flat films. As to the size of camera, the $\frac{1}{4}$ plate is by far the most useful, being right for lantern slides and large enough for most objects. Enlargements can be made to double size (or whole plate) quite as good as collotype or net will reproduce them. The time and work of using a whole-plate size are scarcely ever repaid by the results for practical archaeology.

The fashion of wide-angle lenses is useless for everything excepting architecture at close quarters. And for most objects it is very detrimental to have so short a focus, as it distorts and spoils the perspective. It is best to use too long a focus in order to get truer views of objects, at least 6 inches focus for a $\frac{1}{4}$ plate. There does not seem to be any appreciable gain in the newer patterns of lenses over the older " rapid rectilinear " or " symmetrical " ; and the positive disadvantages of some recent lenses are seen in the smaller aperture and lack of light for focussing, and the distortion at extreme edges. The iris diaphragm is a disadvantage, as it brings in another variable, while the time of exposure can be varied to any extent needed. It is best to stick to

Fig. 38. Throwing sand ; drop-shutter view. | Fig. 39. Girls at rest ; diagonal mirror view.

one small stop, say $f/100$, and learn exposures
entirely on that basis ; then in case of poor light
a larger stop, as $f/25$ or $f/8$, can be used proportion-
ately to shorten the time. Small stops can be made
out of a strip of tin plate or blackened card ; and
the hand camera can be stopped down with a pin-
hole stop stuck in front of the lens so as to work
at almost any nearness and scale with exposures of
$\frac{1}{2}$ or 1 minute in full sunshine.

The instantaneous shutter is a useless article for
all fixed objects. It is far better to work with a
small stop which gives plenty of depth of focus, and
expose for 2 to 20 seconds, which is long enough
for $f/100$ on slow plates in Egypt. For direct enlargement of objects a stop of $f/200$ is excellent,
and only needs 30 seconds exposure. If a shutter
is wanted a simple drop can easily be extemporised
(Fig. 38) fitting on to the front of the lens, and
such will give fine results. A diagonal mirror front
can be made out of any decent scrap of looking-
glass, without showing any double image (Fig. 39).

Rapid films are another fashion better avoided,
as for fixed objects there is no great hurry. The
slowest films made have never caused any practical
inconvenience in my work, and they are far safer
to keep and to develop. The skew-back is never
needed except for architecture ; and in the few cases
where it is necessary, the effect can always be as
well obtained by taking the plate square, and then
copying it skewed in a skew-back camera. The
sliding and rising front is about the only complication that is useful in serious work ; and if a long
focus lens is used a large amount of slide can be

obtained; but a camera with a free-swinging lens turning to any angle would be the best form.

The preparation of the object is a very important point. Any sunk carving or inscription of small size

Preparing objects.
should generally be filled in with whiting (Fig. 41) or charcoal dust, according as the material is dark or light, so as to give a strong contrast (Fig. 40). In case of worn inscriptions on impervious stone, such as rock crystal, the lines may be marked with China ink, dried on, and then gently wiped with damp fingers until only the faint hollows retain the ink. What is hardly visible to the eye can thus be brought up clearly. If hollows are slight and smooth, so that they will not hold a powder, brush over with stiff paste, wipe the face clean on a damp handkerchief, and then press in the powder. Only rather coarse powders should be used, in order to avoid staining the object. In field-work objects should also be carefully dressed. Reliefs upon weathered stones (Fig. 37) should be dusted over with sand, and then lightly wiped until just the wrought relief is cleared, and the ground is left smoothed with sand. Stones in building should be brushed or scraped clean, so as to contrast with the earth. Joints in walls should be picked out or brushed so as to show clearly. Sometimes, as in a flooring of wood (Fig. 42), the whole should be entirely brushed clean, and then the joints packed with the lightest-coloured sand so as to contrast well. A grave needs hand-picking, and then every bone brushing clean, and the ground between packing with dark earth to give contrast. All pottery and objects should be entirely cleaned around, and lifted

Fig. 40. Ivory tablet of Zer;
light half with black,
dark half with white.

Fig. 41. Bronze hypocephalus,
XXX Dyn. ;
filled in with white.

DRESSING TOMBS FOR PHOTOGRAPHING.

Fig. 42. Wooden floor of Azab. | Fig. 43. Naqada, prehistoric.

slightly so as to show a clear outline. The proper dressing of a grave (Fig. 43) will easily occupy two hours of work. Nothing which adds to the contrast and clearness of an object should be neglected. Sometimes for dark objects it is well to dust them with very fine white powder, as with a puff-ball, so as to give some light on the darker sides. And for objects of mottled colour, such as carved porphyry, a coat of flake-white water-colour is best, so as to show the relief only and not the colour. For coins and gems there is no method to compare with photographing from plaster casts, which are always used in serious work.

The lighting is the most important element in photographing. No other requirement is so essential, for with bad lighting nothing can be done. The rule of the light coming Lighting. from the top left hand should always be followed where no special direction is needed. Generally a diagonal light is best for inscriptions, as most lines are vertical or horizontal. An object should first be held with a moderately oblique light on the face of it, then quickly revolved in the plane of its face, so as to see the changing effect of light from different directions, observing what lines disappear in various positions, and selecting the most effective direction. On setting it up, with the sun (or other light) in the best direction, the obliquity of the light should then be tried, tilting the object more or less, until the details are sufficiently shown without too heavy shadows. In case of a human face the light should be nearly vertical, and the obliquity of it sufficient to bring out the cheek curves to the best. Of course, the position of the object must be regulated entirely by the direction of the light, and a figure may need to be tilted in any position. A conical or cylindrical object must be placed with its axis pointing a little behind or below the light, so as to lighten the whole side. For fixed objects, such as buildings, a time-table of the best hours for each part should be drawn up and followed.

Beside direct lighting, subsidiary lighting is very useful. Any dark shadows should be lighted with reflectors of white paper or card, or actual mirror. Or during an exposure of several seconds, or more, a transient mirror reflection can be played about the shadow, so as not to show an edge to the light. When looking at the image on the ground glass each part should be searched to see if any detail is lost by shadow, or if an outline is lost against an equally dark background; if so, some difference of lighting must be made. Various slips of card may be fixed around the object, so as to cast shadows which will make some part of a brightness differing from its background, and other slips to cast lights on any dead part. For photographing an ebony statuette (Fig. 44) I searched in the camera for each dead uniform surface, and then fixed a slip of card so as to break the deadness with a reflection; half a dozen such slips, at a foot or two distance, left the figure without a single curve not brought out and intelligible.

Reflectors are also very useful for lighting dark subjects. Three or four sheets of tin plate should have the edges turned up to stiffen them, and be of slightly different sizes so as to nest together for

LIGHTING BY REFLECTION.

Fig. 44. Ebony negress.　XVIII Dyn. | Fig. 45. Tomb of Sem-nefer.　Gizeh.

carrying.   One planted in the sunshine outside a
tomb will send a beam in, which may be reflected
again by another.   With three successive reflections,
round two right angles, I have lighted an entirely
dark chamber (Fig. 45) enough to photograph with
five minutes exposure and full aperture.   The
successive reflections so neutralise each other's variations that a very uniform lighting results.

If a flat surface with different colour is the object,
then a light exactly from behind the camera is best,
so as to avoid any shadows.   A faint ink-writing on
rough pottery will appear with a back light when it
seems quite hopeless in a side light.   For papyri two
equal electric arc lights are placed, one on each side
of the camera, so that there can be no shadows and
no reflections.

Backgrounds should be considered.   For most
objects there is nothing so good as black velvet, as
a long exposure can be taken so as to <small>Arrangement</small>
bring out the shadows on the object, <small>of objects.</small>
without any glare from the background.   The
ground should extend far beyond the object, as any
bright surface near the object may make internal
reflections in the camera.   In short, no bright
surface should be visible within 60° of the axis of
the lens.   For dark objects of which the outline
alone is important a light ground might be used;
though even here probably a black ground and long
exposure would be better.   A glass background with
light or dark surface some distance behind it is used
sometimes, so as to avoid all shadows from objects.
But in many cases a shadow is positively useful,
and adds to the intelligibility of the view.

The direction of the camera is too often horizontal. For portable objects a vertical position is generally better, and for groups it is essential (Fig. 46). The background on which the objects are laid can be tilted so as to get oblique light from sun or window, and the camera tilted equally from the vertical by shifting the legs. Scraps of wax can be stuck on below objects, so as to keep them in any exact position required for lighting or viewing, or scraps of charcoal used as wedges which do not show on the black backing. There is no need to trouble about depth of focus, as the insertion of a small stop, as $f/100$, is enough to bring up every part sharp. I have taken a bracelet (Fig. 47) with the sides at 7 and 9 inches from the lens both in perfectly sharp focus. In fact, a subject may be contracted into the plate by putting it out of focus, and then focussed by the stop. For all cases of large-scale photographs or enlargements it is best to focus by shifting the distance from object to lens, and not from lens to plate.

In setting up the camera everything should be done as far as possible before looking into it,—the distance measured for the scale required, the camera set square with the plane of the object in both directions, and set so as to have the object upright on the plate. All of this can be far better dealt with from outside. The actual focussing and slight adjustments can then be done when viewing the ground glass. For skew positions it is best to hold the camera in the hand where it ought to be, keeping the legs turned up from the ground ; and then drop the legs one after another, so as to touch the ground

Fig. 46. Foundation deposit,
laid out horizontally.

Fig. 47. Bracelet of King Zer,
7 and 9 ins. from lens.

or some object ; thus the camera will be left standing in the required position.   The stand should not
have the legs packed by folding sideways ; but they
should be capable of being shortened to the single
length while fixed to the camera, as it is often needful to support it only a foot from the ground.   A
stand should be so made as to give the greatest
range of height.   A common fault of beginners is
not covering the plate, but letting the image be
smaller than necessary.   Unless working to some
uniform scale, an object should be shown as large as
the plate allows ; always remembering that a lantern
slide will seldom take more than 3 inches diameter,
and hardly a full 3 inches square.   It is convenient
to fill a $\frac{1}{4}$ plate with a group, of which the least
important objects are at the sides, and so can be
omitted in a lantern-slide print.   A most troublesome matter is taking a series of wall scenes so that
they will fit exactly together at the edges.   Probably it pays best to do them approximately in the
field, and then enlarge in a copying camera on to a
ruled ground, and so remove all irregularities of
scale and of skewness.   For working to a uniform
scale it is best to fix it by keeping the focal length
unchanged and measuring the distance of the camera
from the object, and not to refer to the size on the
glass.

Stereographic views are most useful for confused
masses of objects, such as a field of ruins.   And if
there are no moving parts there is no   Stereographs.
need to take them simultaneously.   By
shifting the camera to one side, and taking a second
plate, a perfect stereograph is obtained ; and where-

ever the chance is not to be repeated, and two plates are taken to ensure success, a shift should be made so that both may be used together. The amount of shift varies with the distance ; for near objects the distance between the eyes, $2\frac{1}{2}$ or 3 inches, may suffice ; for a general view a foot or 2 feet is better, so as to give more solidity than is naturally seen. Small objects must not be shifted by rotating the object if there are sharp shadows, as such are falsified by the turning ; otherwise a slight twist of the object does for the second view.

It is undesirable to leave developing till long afterwards. In general all negatives should be developed the evening after they are exposed ; thus the future exposures can be regulated, any defective plates can be repeated, and deterioration and risks due to keeping are avoided. In the variety of developers the old pyrogallic acid remains still one of the most reliable. The fanciful instructions about proportions are exploded at once by a glance at the table compiled by Captain Abney. By adopting the mean proportions of all the makers, which is 1 soda carbonate, 1 soda sulphite, and 20 water, as a stock solution, and adding about 3 grains per $\frac{1}{4}$ plate of pyrogallic when using, very uniformly good results are obtained with short exposures. Of course long exposures require bromide ; but that is very seldom needful. Extra local developing by tilting the dish, or painting with a brush, is useful in case of shadows. Tabloid developers are best avoided, as they cause delay in dissolving ; and made-up solutions are cumbrous and expensive. The quantities needed can always

Developing.

be put out by guess, taking $\frac{1}{4}$ of an 8-ounce bottle at a time of soda salts, and weighing pyrogallic for once to know the look of it. For hyposulphite of soda fill the bottle $\frac{1}{3}$ full of crystals, and fill up with water. If a less strong and more graded picture is needed then glycin seems preferable to pyrogallic acid.

No dark room is needed ; developing can always be done in the evening. A red paper envelope split at the bottom and put round the chimney of an ordinary lamp, will best screen the light. The diffused light of a room will not hurt slow plates in developing, and a sheet of brown paper over each tray makes all safe. A first soak in weak pyrogallic solution, to flatten the films, is best before developing. For washing where water may be scarce it suffices to have a row of six soup plates of water, and to pass each film through each plate for five minutes, so completing the washing of each in half an hour. A zinc box with 6 or 8 divisions, shifting the negatives forward through each division, will also work well. For drying it is best to have a row of pins along the edge of a shelf, and then to punch out a small hole in a corner of the film and hang it up, with the gelatine face under the shelf to keep dust from it. A dusty evening in Egypt will leave each film like a piece of sandpaper ; and in case of this the films can be afterwards rapidly washed under a stream of water, wiping with a lump of cotton-wool. This will be enough without resoaking the film. Owing to the dryness of the air in Egypt films generally curl up in drying, and if forcibly flattened they are liable to strip. They are best packed in lots of about 50, coiled up together as a cylinder, and wrapped in a turn of paper. When in England they can be flattened out by being left near an open window in damp weather, or dipped in water and left to dry. For quick drying, films may with care be stood inside a fender before a fire, and finished over a lamp chimney. I have thus dried them in about twenty minutes.

CHAPTER VIII

PRESERVATION OF OBJECTS

THE preservation of the objects that are found is a
necessary duty of the finder. To disclose things
only to destroy them, when a more skilful or patient
worker might have added them to the world's
treasures, is a hideous fault. And the excavator
must be ready for all emergencies, for all classes of
objects in all stages of decay, and deal with each
without delays, and often with scanty and unsuitable
means at hand for their treatment. Some familiarity
with chemistry and physics and properties of materials,
is one of the first requisites for an excavator. All
this applies in a lesser degree to the difficulties of
transport, which is also part of the preservation of
the antiquities.

As conditions so infinitely vary it is useless to
lay down any fixed rules for treatment. Such rules
would hinder the use of common sense, which is
essential to success. But examples of how different
materials are affected, and how difficulties have been
met, will lead to the excavator thinking out a fit
treatment for each case as it arises. In all this we
are stating field practice only, and not dealing with

museum methods, which differ by having far more
command of resources, and by not having to deal
with any of the troublesome cases which do not
survive to reach a museum.

The great enemy of stonework is salt.   In
Egypt this permeates the soil so that nothing is free

Stone.   from it ; and any object near the surface
has   much   salt   accumulated   in   it   by
evaporation.   The effect of salt is to disintegrate
the stone, and make it flake or fall away in powder.
If there is the faintest taste of salt on a stone slab
it should be laid to dry, face down, on the ground ;
for I have seen a fine block of sculpture entirely
destroyed by being left for a single day face upward.
When the stone is once dry it is safe in Egypt, but
in a damp country it may begin a course of slow
destruction by continual recrystallization of salt.
Sculptures have been entirely wrecked by being
cemented into the wall of a museum ; the wet of
the cement brought all the salt to the face and
ruined it.   The only treatment for salt in stone or
any other material is long soaking in water.   If a
canal is at hand, stones may be sunk in it for some
weeks, face down.   Or barrels or zinc trays may be
used, and the water changed every two or three
days, for five or six times.   After such soaking the
stone must be left to dry face down, so that all the
remaining salt will come out on the back.   Where
there is not much salt it would be best to lay the
stone back upwards to dry, brush off any salt which
comes out, and then wet the ground below, so that
more water may be drawn up to evaporate on the
back.   If this was continued until no salt appeared

the stone would be cleaned, and the face could not be injured. Sometimes a face is already flaking, and then the stone must be kept quite flat in soaking and drying, so that each flake will be left in place, and can be stuck down afterwards. Granite is often entirely disintegrated into separate crystals, if it has lain near the surface. It is then even impossible to turn the block over to copy it, as there is no cohesion left in the mass. The only salvation possible for such a block would be to make a thick plaster or cement coat to the exposed parts, under cut, and turn the whole over with a board beneath it, and then saturate it hot with paraffin wax.

The face of limestone is often in tender condition, and will not bear wet brushing to clean it. Dry picking and brushing is then the only resource. If long exposed to damp, limestone dissolves throughout the body of it, so that it becomes spongy, and like putty with the contained water. A large sarcophagus lid in this state at Denderah was brought up to the house, then covered with 3 or 4 inches of sand, and left to dry slowly for some weeks; otherwise it would have cracked to chips by contraction on the face. When quite dry it was very porous, but in safe state for copying and transport. I have seen a slab of limestone in perfect condition, reduced to a shapeless paste by a few minutes of sharp rain.

The original stucco facing often remains on limestone, and also the colour. If the carving has been fine it is best to remove the stucco, which is generally much less detailed. But if the stucco is an improvement on the carving, and especially if there is colour, it must be preserved. This is best done by fixing it with thin tapioca water, just so thick that it will soak into the stone without leaving any glair when dry. This treatment also does for limestone with a rotten face.

The same tapioca water may be used for fixing colours on stucco, as I did on the Tell el Amarna pavement (Fig. 48); and the thickness must be graduated to the porosity, so that it will just soak entirely into the material. Any film left on the face will peel away.

Pottery has not much to fear except salt, and that should be soaked out as from stone. Glazed pottery with salt in it is more difficult to clear, as it takes so long to get any change in and out of it. But a persistent soaking will clear it in the course of some weeks; and, if necessary, partly drying it in intervals, will bring the salt out of the cracks, whence it can be dusted off. The commonest failing of glazes is decomposition. The green turn brown, by the decomposition of the iron from green silicate to brown oxide; and this may take place from the porous interior without breaking the external face. The blue glazes go white; and this can be partly remedied by warming and soaking with paraffin wax, which fills the fine cracks and displays the remaining colour again. Sometimes the outer coat of clear glaze over faience inlay is decomposed, without spoiling the faience below. In this case it is like a picture of which the varnish is gone brown,—it only needs cleaning. The decomposed glaze can be scraped off, or rubbed with fine emery paper, until the faience is clean, and

Pottery.

FRESCOES, TELL EL AMARNA.

Fig. 48. Plants and animals.   Fig. 49. The two princesses.

then a coat of paraffin wax clears the colour and preserves it from decomposition. When glazed ware, especially of the earliest times, is first found, it is very tender and soft. It then needs the most careful handling, and must not be brushed or cleaned until it is quite dry and hardened.

Textiles are also often saturated with salt, especially the Coptic garments which are in graves near the surface. They may be safely soaked to remove the salt and the organic *Textiles.* matter, and then dried by pressing in a towel and laying between sheets of paper. The most tender examples might perhaps be best treated by placing with half a dozen sheets of blotting-paper over and under, and keeping wet below while evaporating on the top ; this would carry the salt out to the top of the blotting paper. In any long soaking of organic stuffs a little carbolic acid is desirable, to prevent souring and putrefaction of the material. In every case the threads of textiles are liable to crumble, and any great amount of washing will tend to reduce a good deal to powder. Ironing is always desirable to consolidate the stuff.

Wood does not suffer so much from salt as from rot and white ants. Any salt may be soaked out ; or, if the wood is tender and will not bear that, a very stiff jelly should be *Wood.* made, so that it will just melt at boiling : the wood dropped in when the jelly liquefies, and left in the jelly cold for a week or two. Then the salt will dialyse out into the jelly, without any free water softening the wood. On remelting the jelly the wood can be removed, and the salt will be left in the jelly.   The gelatine will strengthen and improve the wood.   This process can be used excellently for ivories or bones, which would be ruined by soaking in water.   Whole skeletons can be set in stiff size, and taken out weeks after, freed from salt, as was done to those from Medum, now in the College of Surgeons.

Rotted wood is very tender to handle ; and from its continued contraction when exposed to the air it will fall to pieces.   If nearly dry, but rotted, the best safeguard is to coat it with beeswax or paraffin wax ; if it can be lifted threads can be slipped round it, and the whole dipped in hot wax until soaked. Or it may have a rapid coat of wax chilled upon it, which protects it and binds it together for travelling, and which can be soaked into it by piecemeal heating afterwards.   If the wood will not bear lifting, it may be coated by dashing on superheated paraffin wax almost at boiling-point.   This will soak deep into the wood like hot water, and consolidate it so that it can be moved quite safely.   The same processes apply also to stuccoed wood, which needs such safeguards, as otherwise the stucco all falls off by the continued shrinkage of the wood.   The great stuccoed sarcophagus at Hawara was preserved by heating the surface with a wire dish of charcoal burning about six inches above it, and flooding the surface with melted wax so soon as it was enough heated to absorb it.   Perhaps superheated paraffin wax would have carried enough heat with it to soak in without the charcoal fire.   For all heating of wax it is best to use a cast-iron saucepan, as soldered tins may give way before the wax boils.   Another

treatment, especially suited for large objects, is painting with several coats of wax dissolved in benzol.

Wood which is very wet is more difficult to
manage. It may be kept for long under water, like
the wood from the Glastonbury lake village. And
it may be consolidated with silicate solution, as has
been well done in examples from Silchester. Or it
may be removed from water and laid in glycerine
with the top exposed ; thus the water will evaporate
and diffuse, and glycerine take its place.

Ivory is mainly liable to flaking, especially if in
wet soil. When any ivory is seen not in a firm
condition, the earth should be carefully
worked round so as to find the limits of   Ivory.
the ivory, be it a single piece or a collection together.
Then the mass should be under-cut down to a firm
stratum, and lifted out in a whole block of earth.
This should be left to dry slowly ; and after a week
or two the earth should be gently brushed away with
a camel-hair brush, aided by picking with a stout pin.
As each piece of ivory is seen it should be carefully
followed, and if quite dry it may probably be removed entire. If still liable to flake, it can then be
soaked in melted paraffin wax. If the ivory is too
rotted to be detached from the earth, then the whole
mass would have to be baked to rather over blood
heat, and saturated with paraffin wax. After that it
could be safely dissected by careful picking. In
case of finding large groups of ivories in the ground,
too extensive to take out in a block to dry, probably
it would do to isolate them, then lay a few inches of
sand on the top, and light a fire over them : after
slow burning for a few days the ground would be

baked dry below, and could be saturated with wax before lifting the mass.

It sometimes happens that ivories in wet soil get concreted crystalline carbonate of lime upon them, which is much harder than the ivory. This being crystalline is not saturated with wax when the ivory is so treated. Hence after waxing the ivory the surface should be cleaned with benzol or ether on cotton-wool, and then painted with nitric acid to dissolve the crystalline lime. Even strong nitric acid will only dull the surface of waxed ivory, and not remove any perceptible amount, while it dissolves the concretion rapidly. Probably the darkening of the ivory caused by soaking in wax can be mainly removed by heating fuller's earth to over boiling-point, and then rapidly packing the ivory in the earth and pressing it : the heat would melt the wax on the surface, it will be absorbed by the earth, and the face of the ivory will be left dry of wax. The ivories from Nineveh were solidified with gelatine ; but that would probably break up very tender ivories by the amount of water. In case however of much salt in ivory the best way to treat it is to drop it in stiff hot gelatine, cool it, and let it lie in the consolidated mass for a week or two, for the salt to dialyse out. Another way, if the mass is not much cut into hollows, is to lash the ivory closely with thread or fine twine, and then soak it in water to remove the salt ; the twine prevents it falling to pieces, and it can be dipped in wax when dry, and the twine removed.

Papyri require most careful treatment at every stage. They are often found in a very fragile state, and if the roll has to be carried without special pack-

ing in wool it is best to wrap it in a damp handkerchief at once. For unrolling rolls, or
flattening out crushed papyri, damping is
needful. There is no need to steam them, as has
been done in museums. By dipping a towel or
handkerchief in water, and wringing it as dry as
possible, there is enough moisture to penetrate to a
papyrus closely wrapped in it. If there were many
turns then carbolised water would be best, so as to
avoid any decomposing during a long penetration of
the damp. Usually a single night is enough for
damping through half a dozen folds or turns, enough
to render the papyrus quite pliable. It can then be
unrolled, or uncreased with the fingers ; and as each
inch of it is laid flat it should be secured by turning
down newspaper or blotting-paper over it and sliding
a board or book over the flattened part. After leaving it between a dozen leaves of paper to absorb
the moisture for some days under pressure it is dry
and firm. Small pieces can well be carried in books,
and larger sheets in piles of paper between boards.
When the papyrus is too rotted to be damped, as
the crossed layers of it would part, then it can only
be cut to pieces with a sharp penknife at every fold
and turn ; and each piece fastened down on a sheet
at once in place. This was the only possible way
to open the great Ptolemaic revenue papyrus over
40 feet long ; even a single turn of the roll needed
to be cut into dozens of pieces.

For fastening down papyrus it is fatal to gum or
paste it on to a sheet of card, as the gradual contraction of the gum will break up the layers of the
papyrus. The safest way of all for very rotted

papyri is to rub a sheet of glass with beeswax, lay the papyrus on it, and press with a warm hand until it sticks to the wax ; then cover with another sheet of glass. For ordinary firm papyri minute spots of paste, as small as possible, should be put at every inch or two round the edges, and farther apart in the middle ; then a sheet of thin soft paper should be pressed on it, to serve as a backing. Thus there is no wide space pasted which can contract in future ; and even if the papyrus has to be remounted the paper can be torn to pieces behind it. The sheet of mounting paper should be fixed under glass. But it is a mistake to attach card to glass round the edges, as it bags away by damp and warping, and leaves a large air space, which is very detrimental. It is best to place the mounting paper between two sheets of glass ; or, for the sake of lightness and safety, the back may be of thin picture-back-board, well baked dry, and free from cracks and knots. For fastening the edges thin leather or linen may be glued around.

Dealing with carbonised papyri is an art in itself. So far as field work goes the main work is to remove the earth entirely from the top of the papyrus, so as to leave no weight upon it : then under-cut, and take out the whole lump, with a block of earth under it. The papyri must then, in the house, be carefully separated, one document from another, by splitting apart and lifting with an ivory paper knife or blunt table knife, the lighter the better, so as to feel the way with it. Each separate roll should then be wrapped in soft paper (never cotton-wool) and packed a few together, in small tin boxes. Thus they will travel safely and without loss. The museum work is outside of our scope ; but broadly the Neapolitan plan of holding the pieces in place with adhesive paper on the back is not so good as separate treatment of each piece, laying it down in position on a sheet of glass with small touches of paste, or perhaps pressing it on to waxed glass like the rotted papyri. Burnt papyri are read by the difference of reflection of the surface, and hence must be viewed with light from behind the eye, or light reflected by a mirror placed almost between the eye and the papyrus.

Bead-work is often found in a state in which it cannot be moved owing to rotting of the threads. Elaborate decoration with the winged scarab, four genii, inscriptions, etc., is Bead-work. found on mummies of about the XXVth Dynasty. But, if the threads are decayed, the beads are merely lying in position, and will fall away if the mummy be tilted or shaken. In such a case I have opened the wooden coffin very gently, cutting out the pegs by which it was fastened. Having melted a pot of wax on a stove in the tomb, I then dashed spoonfuls of it over the beads ; it needs to be thrown sharply, so as to splash out, or it runs off all in one line. The wax must be only just barely liquid, or it will penetrate to below the beads. When a sheet of wax is thus put over all the beads, the sheet may be lifted up, and the pattern is seen in a clean condition, reversed on the under side. The sheet can then be fixed with more wax into a tray of wood, so as to keep it safely. If any of the beads are not firm they can be heated and pressed farther into the wax. Strings of beads are seldom found with the thread

strong enough to hold together. The earth should
be loosened with a penknife, and blown away, so as to
disclose as long a line as possible, then the order of
the beads should be noted for restringing them, in
the original pattern.   The tracing out and noting of
a string of beads in a grave may often occupy an
hour or two hours, keeping the face close to the
ground so as to blow the dust away exactly, without
disturbing the beads.

Stucco on wood we have already noticed, under
the preservation of wood.   However firm the stucco

Stucco.

may seem at first, the gradual contraction
of the wood will make it fall away ; but
when once saturated with paraffin wax, this movement is stopped, and the stucco is held on to the
basis.

Stucco on mud bricks is a difficult material to
preserve.   Three instances may be given of dealing
with it.   Where the coat was a mere whitewash on
mud plastering, as at Tell el Amarna (Fig. 49), I
removed the bricks behind it by cutting them gently
to pieces with a chisel ; thus the coat of mud plaster
was left standing up a foot or more in air, although
it was entirely friable owing to white ants having
eaten out the straw from it.   Then placing a box lid
covered with sheets of paper against the face, it was
firmly grasped behind, and turned over with the lid
to support it, face down.   Lying on the box lid it
was taken to the house ; a frame of parallel bars of
wood was made, each an inch wide and an inch
apart ; each bar was coated with mud-and-sand
mortar, and then the frame was pressed gently on
the back of the fresco, and puddled in with mortar

between the bars. On then reversing the frame and box lid, the fresco was left resting on the frame, with a bedding which was perfectly true, and incapable of warping or contraction. To pack this a sheet of cotton wool was placed on the face, a thin board cut to size placed over this, and string lashed tightly round the face board and notches in the ends of the frame bars. In this state it travelled quite safely, although the material was so tender that a finger would push through it anywhere ; this was illustrated by a museum attendant at Cairo, when ordered to carry one of the frames of fresco.

Where the stucco is thicker, about $\frac{1}{16}$ inch, but wholly shattered into minute chips, none over $\frac{1}{4}$ inch across, a different treatment was necessary, as at Medum. The mass of plaster and stucco was laid face down, the mud cut away behind it till about a square inch of shattered plaster was bared at the back ; this was covered with a thin coat of fresh plaster (mixed in the palm of the hand) ; then another square inch was bared and coated, and so on, until the whole of the mud was removed and the old stucco all lay smeared with a thin coat of fresh plaster on the back. A large slate was then cut to size ; a pudding of liquid plaster was poured on to the stucco and pressed out as thin as could be with the slate. When it was set, the old painted stucco was thus securely cemented on to the slate ; light, tough, and portable, it travelled to America in perfect state.

The third method is where the surfaces are curved. By cutting away the back as thin as is safe, and setting in a firm backing of cement, even this

H

difficult subject may be dealt with, and removed safely.

Metals do not require much treatment in the field ; but it is needful to understand the condition of them in order to know how they can be safely treated. Gold should be cleaned as little as possible, as the old red surface is the best appearance of it ; a little brushing with camel-hair brush and plain water to remove the dust is generally enough. Where there is much silver in it, as in electrum, the surface is dark with chloride of silver ; this may be removed with strong ammonia or cyanide of potassium. Gold-foil often requires straightening out into its former shape, but it must not be burnished in so doing, as that expands the form.

Gold.

Silver is one of the most troublesome metals, as it is so very readily attacked by chlorine and sulphur ; and, moreover, it undergoes a colloidal rearrangement by which it breaks readily into irregular curved grains, and it is in this state as rotten as rotten brass. If deeply corroded nothing can well be done to it ; the lumpy crust shows more of the original form than the metal would show if bared. When the corrosion is but slight it may be removed, either by solution in strong ammonia or cyanide of potassium, or by reduction. To bring the chloride into the state of porous metal, it is only needful to place it with zinc or iron in a solution of salt or weak vinegar or lemon juice, and in a few hours the whole of the chlorine has gone over to the fresh metal. The powdery silver left can be mainly brushed away in water, and a little picking with a bone point will loosen it entirely. Of course, the

Silver.

whole of the silver removed has come out of the body of the metal, which is left porous and tender, although the face may be unbroken. It will not bear, therefore, the same cleaning as new and strong metal. In the case of silver coins in fine condition, each coin should be reduced separately, and the whole of the old silver weighed with it before cleaning it away, so as to recover the original weight. Silver must never be put bare in a tin box, as the chlorine forms chloride of tin, which deliquesces, and then attacks the iron and stains the silver with brown rust. Often there is both chloride and lime on the surface, and alternations of ammonia and weak acid are required for cleaning.

Copper objects are distinguished from bronze by retaining usually their pliability. This renders them much easier to clean, as they are seldom deeply corroded, and the red oxide upon Copper. them will generally flake off clean by blows, and leave the original face in perfect condition. A very light hammer should be used, and sharp scaling blows be given, so as to flake off even half-an-inch breadth of scale at once, without ever touching the old face. In hollows which cannot so easily be struck, an iron nail may be used as a punch, and struck so as to crush the red oxide little by little. A copper object which scales freely is a treat to clean, as the old face can be entirely bared, and appears of a beautiful red-brown colour with all the detail quite perfect. Very thin copper may, however, have entirely passed into green carbonate, if buried in a damp soil; and in this case nothing can be done except washing off the earth and dirt.

Bronze and brass need much more care than copper, as they contain a mixture of alloys of very **Bronze.** different oxidability ; hence much of the material all through the mass will have moved up to the surface and been corroded there, while the form and size of the original may at present contain only half the metal in a very porous and brittle condition.   In some cases bronzes may be scaled by blows like copper, and they then appear in their best condition.   But more often they are too brittle, or the corrosion adheres too tightly, for it to be thus removed.   For cleaning off small quantities of green carbonate, vinegar left to stand for some days does well.   But the proper solvent of both carbonate and oxide is dilute hydrochloric acid, about 1 to 10 or 20 of water, as this will not attack the metal, but only the corroded parts.   The objection to this solvent is that it leaves a thick mud of white oxy-chloride of copper, which is difficult to brush off, and which stains the skin green in handling.   The treatment is to brush off as much as can be easily removed, and then pickle in hyposulphite of soda, which dissolves the white coat ; if used hot and strong this will clean the metal to a bright metallic condition.   After all these solutions, a long washing in many waters for two or three days is needed to remove all trace of salts which might afterwards make further corrosion.   Minute traces of chlorides are specially dangerous, as they decompose with carbonic acid in the air, forming carbonate, and liberating the chlorine to attack more metal ; thus a trace of chloride will eat through any amount of copper.   The extent to which bronzes should be cleaned, should be ruled by the fullest display of original workmanship: so long as more detail can be shown more crust should be removed. But, if possible, some of the coat of red oxide should be left on plain parts as a guarantee of the age of the work. To bare bronzes entirely, and then oil and smoke them, is barbarous treatment, to be seen in some museums. If something is desired over the bare metal, the bronze may be left in a shallow pan of water, soaking for some weeks, by which it will gain a tinge of red oxide over it which is suitable and pleasing. Another mode of scaling is to heat the bronze over a fire or in melted lead, and then plunge in cold water, which loosens the scale from it. It often happens that a bronze has the original face broken up by corrosion, and then no cleaning is of any use, the mass of green carbonate shows more than any other surface would do. This last and worst state is indicated by cracks in the outer coat, due to further expansion of the inner body. A cracked bronze is best left alone.

A frequent disease of bronzes is the formation of small granules of translucent bright green rust. This is attributed to an organic growth, which is infectious, and may spread through a collection. One of the worst instances I dipped in carbolic acid, and this absolutely stopped the attack, proving that it is not due to action of chlorine. But we must not take this as a certain proof of the organic nature of the mischief, in view of the inhibitory effect of anæsthetics, etc., in stopping electric and chemical action.

Lead is usually coated with white carbonate, the

outer face of which shows more than the metallic
surface beneath. It should therefore be
let alone ; but if it shows signs of further
changes, due to salts in it acting with damp, then
soaking in several waters will probably make it safe.
If carbonate continued to be formed, I should try
saturating with paraffin wax.

Lead.

Iron can seldom be cleaned ; but if it has only a
little superficial rust, this may be removed by placing
it in the strongest nitric acid, which dissolves the oxide but renders the iron
passive.   For ordinarily rusted iron all that can be
done is to arrest further changes.   A long soaking
in water to remove all salts, and then baking dry
and saturating with wax, is a safe treatment and
always available.

Iron.

Sorting and joining fragments is sometimes very
essential.   In the royal tombs of the Ist Dynasty
we collected thousands of pieces of stone
bowls and vases.   Only a very small
number out of such cartloads of fragments were of
value as they lay ; but so far as they could be reconstructed they gave an important series of forms.
To extract any result it was needful to place together
all the pieces that belonged to each separate vase ;
and the same work frequently had to be done on
a lesser scale in dealing with groups of broken
stone and pottery.   Taking the whole of the fragments which can be supposed by their position to
belong together, they are first sorted over for quality,
making as many divisions as are quite safe to be
distinguished one from the other, so that there shall
be no chance of parts of one bowl being classed in

Sorting.

two different divisions. All the pieces of one division, sometimes as many as 500 of one quality, are then to be laid out on tables,—the pieces of brim placed at the top of the tables, and classed according to form and curvature; the pieces of middle of the vase along the middle of the table, all carefully laid with the axis vertical; the pieces of base at the nearer edge of the table, classed according to diameter. Taking then the first piece of brim, it is held at each end of each other piece to which it can possibly belong; every possible fit is thus found. Each piece of brim is to be thus tried with all that follow it, those before it having been already tried with it. When all the possible junctions of brim have been made, then a row of joined brim pieces are to be laid on a board, and the angle which each broken edge makes with the vertical is to be looked for among all the broken sides of the middle pieces, looking for such slope at both upper and lower sides if the tops are not distinguishable from the bottoms of the pieces. Thus, say the first broken edge of brim slopes at ⟨ 20°, every piece broken at 20° ⟨ or ⟩ must be compared to see if it will fit. At least twenty different directions of fracture can be mentally distinguished, and the slight curve and irregularities increase this to at least fifty varieties, so that each piece of brim only needs actual touching with about 2 per cent of the pieces of middle. When every possible fit of brim to middle pieces is made, then the bases can be similarly compared, having first fitted them by sorting the curvatures. A load of 500 pieces will take several hours of this sorting, at the end of which every possible fit will have been made.   Not more than half-an-hour or one hour at a time can be usefully given to such sorting, as the eye and attention become too much fatigued to observe the fits.   When finished, all the fragments belonging to one bowl are to be wrapped together, and a number given to the parcel ; and the odd pieces can be thrown away unless worth having singly.   The method for drawing the completed forms has been described in the chapter on drawing.

CHAPTER IX

PACKING

BEFORE packing carved blocks it is generally best to saw off the backs, so as to lighten the quantity. A face should always be sawn from each end up to the middle, leaving it about twice as thick in the middle as at the ends, so as to bear the strain of travelling. If a block is so wide on the face that it is liable to be broken in transit, the best course is to saw it in pieces, cutting from the back through to $\frac{1}{2}$ or 1 inch from the face, and then snapping it, so that the face can be re-joined perfectly. Limestone is sawn with a large rip saw or stonemason's saw, using a hammer and chisel if any flinty portions are met with, and also using some hammer dressing. Soft Silsileh sandstone may be cut with pieces of tin plate, such as petroleum tins or biscuit tins ; or else with a thin strip of wood set with wire nails to serve as teeth of a saw. The harder stones must be moved as found, for the cost of reducing the weight would be more than that of carrying it.

In all questions of packing long objects, it must be remembered that the best points of support for equality of strains are at 21 per cent (say $\frac{1}{5}$) from each end.   Any long stone must therefore be held

Long objects. in its case by cross bars or thicker pads or hay at $\frac{1}{5}$ from each end.   It is impossible to reckon on a case being so rigid, and so perfectly fitting, that it will give uniform support all along, with a much smaller elasticity than that of the stone.   The utmost any case can do for stone is to deaden blows and shocks, and to hold the stone

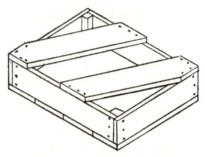

Fig. 50.—Box for flat slab of stone, lid of diagonal bars.

so that it is equally likely to break in the middle or at the supports ; and this is gained by the grip at $\frac{1}{5}$ from each end.   A good packing for small slabs that are not liable to break, is a shallow box (Fig. 50), with the stone face down on dried fodder or straw, and two cross bars parallel and diagonal on the top, to hold the stone in.   Such a box is easily lifted by the bars, saves all Customs examination, and will not tempt thieves.   In all instances remember that it is useless to put general softening round stones in a box.   The best points to take the pressure should be considered, and then thick pads nailed on the box to catch those best points of contact.

The largest stones cannot usefully have any case ; as a case which would not be cracked up by the weight in moving, would be so thick and **Heavy stones.** heavy that it would make the stone far less moveable. If the stone is strong it only needs three or four thicknesses of old clothes and

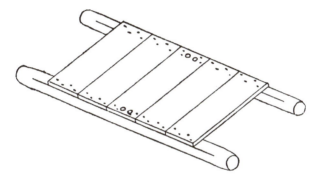

FIG. 51.—Tray for carrying heavy blocks of stone, lashed on by ropes through the holes.

sacking tightly roped on, in order to travel safely. If it has a tender face, a skin of board may be put over that with some cotton-wool padding under the sacking cover. It is best for blocks of 1 to 4 cwt. to make a tray (Fig. 51) with poles projecting a foot at each corner to serve as handles, and then lash the block firmly on the tray. This encourages porters to lift it rather than throw it over. Such things as granite columns or colossi need no cover, but only softening of wood or pads, put under bearing points during moving. On shipboard they travel best laid at the bottom of a cargo of beans in bulk or bales of cotton, which wedge them tight.

Pottery is the most troublesome stuff to pack. The difficulty lies in keeping the packing material at the right places, and preventing it lumping together and so letting the contacts become bare. All the larger hollows must be filled with small pottery, or very light boxes, or empty tins, so that the packing cannot shift together. For large jars it is best to roll up straw in cloth to form cushions 1 to 2 inches thick, and nail these on the box at the points of contact ; always observing if the jar can get loose by skewing into the diagonal. It is often needful to tie cotton stuff over the mouths of jars to prevent the packing working loose into the jar. For flat open forms, such as dishes and wide bowls, a stack should be made with the flattest below, so that each dish rests solely on its centre, and all the edges are free. A very little softening between them, and a firm block (such as a round tin pot) in the top one to take the pressure, will make them all travel with a solid contact right through the centres, so that each brim only carries its own weight. Even thin glass dishes can be packed safely in stacks in this way.

Glazed pottery is sometimes very fragile and full of cracks. To save it from falling apart it should be wound with string crossing diagonally in every direction, as tightly as it can be pulled. This firmly binds the jar so that it cannot fall apart. A couple of inches of tightly rammed softening all round it, will make it then travel quite safely.

The material for packing, or *softening*, varies with

the country and the season. In England there is nothing so good as the fine shavings known as "wood-wool." In Egypt the **Softening.** best stuff is *helbeh*, a dried green crop which is very clinging, and holds in any position in which it is thrust. *Tibn*, or chopped straw, is also useful for ramming tight in small spaces. Firm cushions on fixed bearing points are made by rolling up straw in old cloth, and nailing the edges on the box, so that the pressure can never reach the nails. Rough country cotton can be had, but it is dear; and two or three pounds of prepared cotton wool in sheets should be taken for packing delicate things. Plenty of whitey-brown kitchen paper should be taken for wrapping; and some cartridge paper or brown paper for parcels. Stocks of nested parcel-post boxes are very useful; but sliding lids fall out loose by contraction, and glued joints crack to pieces. The domestic stock of biscuit boxes and food tins of course all come in for varied use.

The making of cases is little understood, and least by professional case-makers. Cases are often supplied in London with the grain entirely running round them, and nothing **Cases.** to prevent their splitting around and dropping in two parts. The most perfect construction is that with the grain running in all three directions (Fig. 52), but such boxes have the disadvantage that the lid cannot be entirely removed. The most practical form is with internal corner-posts, and the sides nailed to these with all the grain running around. First the end boards are nailed on to the corner strips, and then the side boards nailed on. All the nails

should be driven diagonally (Fig. 53), alternately one
way and the other, so that no board can be drawn
off without splitting the wood. And the end nails
should always be close to the edge, and rake deep
down into the corner strip, to avoid splitting the
end ; thus the edge of the board cannot part off

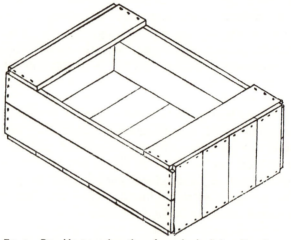

Fig. 52.—Box without cross bars, the grain running in all three dimensions.

with all the lid or bottom nailed to it. For as the
whole weight comes on the last inch of the sides
on to which the bottom is nailed, unless that is well
held on it often parts from the rest of the side. The
lid is of course nailed on with upright nails so as to
draw off; and a large number of short nails, projecting only $\frac{3}{4}$ inch, is the best for this, as if large
nails are used the lid splits during opening and
leaves the nail in the side.

If a case is long, it is best to have some other

upright strips down the sides. Partitions bearing against these strips are good to keep weight from riding down when the box is dropped on one end. If objects vary much in density it is convenient to pack a heavy compartment in the middle and a light one at each end of a case. Any bars or boards used to hold down heavy pieces from shifting

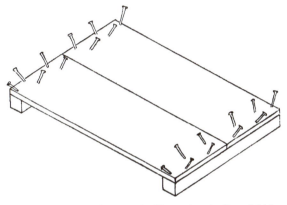

FIG. 53.—End of a box in course of making, to show the diagonal driving of the nails.

should not be nailed through the sides, as damage is often done by the violence needed to loosen them in unpacking. Such bars should be held in place by side strips, or other solid articles in the packing. Tin pots are very convenient to protect small and delicate things, and to hold heavy objects from shifting about.

The packer must always remember that the un-packer will not know the contents of a case, nor any precautions that are needful. The best arrangements, which may seem Unpacking. infallible, may be entirely upset by the unpacker opening the case at the bottom; hence no papers of directions in a case should be relied upon. Also the unpacking is generally left in museums to be done by rough labourers, who may entirely over-look needful precautions or even throw away most valuable things in the boxes. It is dangerous, therefore, to pack small objects in straw; nothing under 100 cubic inches should be put separately in the packing, anything less being put together in paper parcels. It must always be remembered that a careless unpacker may unwrap everything, and throw away the papers; hence no labelling or directions should be solely put on the wrappers. Even labels with objects are not safe; as in several museums the labels have been thrown away, or else stacked in a pile together. Labels should have printed on the back in big red letters, "To be kept with the object." Marking upon each object is necessary, whenever possible. The best way to learn the difficulties and fallacies of packing is to carefully study the causes of any disasters found in the unpacking.

APPENDIX

LIST OF TOOLS, ETC., TO BE PROVIDED FOR WORK

For Excavating.—Crowbars, ropes,[1] large hammers, cold-chisels, stone-saw, saw-files, sieves (fine wire), native sieves.[1]

For Cleaning Objects, etc.—Dusting-brush, nail-brush, tooth-brushes, paraffin wax.

[1] These can be obtained in any Egyptian town.

TRANSPORT IN EGYPT.

Fig. 54. Two Nile boats ;
laden with straw.

Fig. 55. Camels starting at dawn.
The return at noonday.

For Packing.—Paper bags, jewellers' tag labels, reams of kitchen paper, nests of boxes, brush to mark boxes, hammers, saws, chisels, brace and bits, pincers, stout pliers, files, awls, spokeshave, screw-drivers, screws, wire nails,[1] square, hone-stone.

For House.—Locks, hinges, bell.

For Copying and Planning. — Cartridge paper, thin journal paper,[1] rag paper for squeezes, spoke brush, paint brushes for outlines, colours for colour copying, drawing boards (several cheap ones, various sizes), tapes, 2-metre rods for gauging work and planning, prismatic compass, box sextant, vertical mirror level.

---

[1] These can be obtained in any Egyptian town.

CHAPTER X

PUBLICATION

THE final shape of the publication of the record has to be borne in mind in all the progress of it. The
Arrangement. arrangement of the plates must precede the writing of the details of the work. In past generations the ideal was to define in words the conclusions and speculations of an author, and, where unavoidably necessary, to illustrate them by some costly engravings. How inefficient such publication may be, is seen at once in Greenwell's *British Barrows,* a work full of important detail, which has to be painfully understood from hundreds of pages of text, where plans—and little else—are needed. Indeed the only means of using the information is to reconstruct plans from the intricate text. As form can now be almost as cheaply expressed as words, the ideal is widely changed. The reader is to be put first of all in possession of all the facts and materials, and the author's conclusions are only a co-ordination, presented to enable the reader to grasp the material, and to feel clearly the effect of it on his sum of ideas, or organised sense of the nature of things. Hence nowadays the main structure of

a book on any descriptive science is its plates, and the text is to show the meaning and relation of the facts already expressed by form.   The plates, therefore, are the first thing to prepare ; and when they are complete it is time to put in words the conclusions which have been reached.

The orderly arrangement of the material in plates is the first duty.   The drawings are each to be made with the final scale in view, so that the lines may be of proper thickness, Plates. neither faint nor coarse.   The material must be classified according to its nature,—views, plans, inscriptions, sculpture, small objects, pottery, etc.   In each class, the historical order must be followed, objects that are to be compared placed together, and the material arranged in an orderly shape, so that it gives a clear impression, and can be easily found again from memory.   The details of the squareness and alignment of the various drawings on a plate are much more serious than might be supposed ; needless irregularity confuses and disappoints the eye and starves the memory, distinctly detracting from the use and value of the work.   Obviously every object on a plate must have a number for reference ; and in a long series it is best for the numbers to run through several plates ; so that " sealing 157 " or " mark 642 " is a complete reference and definition.   A uniform scale should be used throughout a plate, or a series of the same class, and it should be stated in the heading of the plate. Every plate should have stated in its heading the source, nature, age, and scale of the objects ; for these render reference far easier, and also give a value to loose plates apart from the volume. The use of double-page plates is often desirable, in order to show the whole of a large class at one view; the only drawback to them is that objects are more difficult to find in turning over the leaves. At every point it must be remembered that nearly all foreign students, and most English ones, will know the plates but not the text; that the plates will be the material practically used for comparison, and building up a view of the subject; and therefore that they should be as far as possible self-contained and self-explanatory, with full lettering upom them, and should comprise the main results of the work in diagram. To help reference to the text, the list of plates should have the page references to each plate stated, to show where it is described and dealt with in the text. The facility of using, remembering, and referring to the plates should be the first consideration. It is even well to remember to make the right-hand edge, or outer edge, of each plate the strongest part, with the most striking objects and best arrangement, and let the other edge be a residual, as this ensures the best eye-grasp in turning over the leaves.

The amount of plates must depend upon the subject; but it is none too much if the area of plates is double that of the text, or twice as many plates as there are pages. Folding-out plates should be avoided where possible; a double page on a deep guard, so as to lie flat when the book is opened, is the largest that should be ordinarily used. The most absurdly inconvenient shape is to have wide margins to a plate, and a fold at side and another at base, to make it fit the book. It is best to remedy such folly by taking the plates out, cutting them to book size if margins allow, and resetting without folds. The wild freaks of recent books in Egyptology are incomprehensible. We see some with plates which might be bound with text, yet printed with gigantic margins and issued in an entirely different size, so that they cannot be bound, or even stand on the same shelf with the text ; some plates put on guards of tissue paper, so that they tear out of the book in turning over ; one serial in parts with the plates starting fresh numbers with every separate paper, thus one part has half a dozen " Plate 1 " in it, making printed references to the work quite impossible ; other publications with the plates all renumbered and rearranged after printing, and double references throughout; others with scattered numbers of the plates issued, and intermediate numbers to appear later, after many years or never ; some with plates without any numbers to the objects, and stray references in the text showing that they are usually counted by the author from the base upward, and from right to left. Every absurdity which want of design, forethought, and common sense could perpetrate, seems to be found in these monumental works.

The processes used for plates vary greatly in cost and quality. The cheapest is photo-lithography from line drawings ; but only black and white can be given thus, without any Processes. half-tones, and the illustrations must be all together on a plate, and cannot be placed in the text. Yet as it can be done at less than 2d. a square inch for 250, or 6d. for 2000, it enables a much larger quantity of illustration to be given than would be possible otherwise. Relief process from line drawings costs 4d. a square inch for the blocks alone, without printing on paper ; but as it can be placed with the text and printed together, it has a great advantage, especially for small subjects.

Collotype is next in cost, being 6d. a square inch for 250, or 2s. for 2000, but less than this cost in Germany. It has the same disadvantage in being restricted to whole plates, and not mixable with text, but it gives the half-tones well from photographs, and in fine examples is almost as good as a silver print. The finest I have seen were from Berlin. It is best to supply glass positives to the collotyper, and leave him to make such negatives as may suit him. If negatives are sent they are often destroyed. Net process gives half-tones, though with too coarse a grain for very delicate details. The cost is about double that of relief blocks, but as it reproduces photographs which can be mixed with the text it has an enormous use now, from cheap newspapers up to art publications. A disadvantage is that it requires a highly glazed paper to print upon, such as is unpleasant to read, heavy to hold, and liable to decay. Its duration therefore is distinctly ephemeral.

For special subjects the more costly processes are requisite. Chromo-lithography may be expected to cost about half as much again as photo-lithography for each colour used. As seldom less than four colours are efficient it costs at least six times as much as the line plates ; thus the cheapest colour plate begins at the cost of the best net process ; and it may easily come to three or four times that amount. But probably the three-colour photography will soon abolish chromo-lithography, and work much cheaper, perhaps at three or four times the price of collotype.

The autotype, platinotype, heliogravure, Swan electric engraving, and other processes all have their place for special subjects, but seldom come into the general run of archaeological illustration.

A very successful policy for costly works of research is to issue a magnificent edition for libraries, book - collectors, and rich amateurs ; and then to have a much larger edition, Editions. deficient in a few of the most costly and least necessary plates, sold at a cheap rate for students and the general public. Thus one great work of coloured folio plates costs £20 or 3s. a plate for the complete edition ; whereas with a few plates deficient it is only £6 or 1s. a plate. Thus the cost of production is borne by those who demand magnificence, and the results are yet within reach of students.

Another useful arrangement is to issue a public edition for general reading, and an appendix of extra plates for students, which would overweight a general edition. Thus a 2000 edition of the popular half of the plates may cost £400, and a 250 edition of the students' half of the plates may cost £100, so saving £300, which would be uselessly spent on 1750 copies that are not wanted, and which would only be a dead-weight to the main work.

In arrangement of the text the main necessity is ready reference, and a form which can be remembered. The way to this is by classifying the material, dividing into chapters and paragraphs, each with a title,

and above all making a good index, which ought
to be about a tenth of the length of the
work.   A list of plates should have

page references for each plate.   Remember that
all smaller type, footnotes, and tables are far more
expensive than straightforward printing.

The general nature of the record of results has
been already dealt with under the recording ; and
the need of giving an organic handling of the whole
has been pointed out.

As to publication, if any publisher will undertake to issue a work of research at his own risk, well
and good.   If the author gets a gradually

increasing royalty after the first 100
copies, that is as much as can be expected from this
class of literature.   But in no case have any profit-
sharing agreement.   Usually such a work will have
to be issued at the author's risk, and a few of the
pitfalls of such arrangements may be noted.   Let
the manuscript really be in final condition, down to
every stop, before it goes to the printer ; consider
the details of headlines, paragraphing, insertion of
illustrations, arrangements of any tables or lists,
(counting the letters), and in short leave nothing
undefined.   Have an agreement with the printer for
terms, including an average of, say, two author's
alterations in every page, none to alter the length of
any page : this allows for inevitable small improve-
ments, without leaving an entire uncertainty in the
charges.   Correct the proofs in red for the author's
alterations, in black for the printer's errors.   If
alterations exceed the allowance, reckon on paying
for the resetting of the worst pages, so as to bring

the average to the allowance on the rest. Beside
the contract for printing and binding, have a contract with the lithographer, another with the collotyper, and another with the bookseller, for his terms
of commission on sales. Thus the author knows
exactly where he is, and no unpleasantness can arise
from unexpected charges.

After publication, the binder and plate-printer
should be asked for any blocks used ; and to send
up any "overs" or spoilt plates ; as such are often
valuable afterwards to cut up for special uses,
and may save spoiling copies of the book. All
photographs and drawings supplied to the plate- or
block-maker should also be asked for if not returned
at once.

CHAPTER XI

SYSTEMATIC ARCHAEOLOGY

A SCIENCE can hardly be said to exist until it has a developed system of work, and its possibilities of value for teaching purposes depend entirely on the organization of its methods.
Systems of Work.
Geology was a chaos before the generalisation of the successive order of the strata, and the method of the determination of a stratum by its fossils, gave the subject a working system. Astronomy was a maze until the Newtonian laws produced methods of analysis. Chemistry could not be said to have any methods until the use of the balance and the theory of atomic combination made possible the last century of development. So far, archaeology cannot be said to have systematised any working methods except those of artistic comparison and of epigraphy, and these can only cover a small part of the space and time which need to be studied.

Two general modes of work, however, have been begun, beside that of artistic comparison ; and it only needs that they should be fully carried out in order to produce a thoroughly systematic archaeology. These methods are (1) the complete definition of facts by means of a *corpus* of all known varieties of objects, in terms of which every object can be defined ; and (2) the arrangement of material in its order of development by statistical methods and comparison, which bring out the original sequence of construction. These two methods of work may prove to be, for archaeology, what the balance and atomic theory have been for chemistry,—the necessary foundation for systematic knowledge and exact theory.

The collection of known objects in a *corpus* was well done by the early systematisers, especially Montfaucon ; and though his work is nearly two centuries old, it has not yet been superseded by better productions in every department. Since that appeared, the mass of new material which has been collected, especially in the last fifty years, cannot be mastered by one man, if he is ever to find time for original work ; and the whole subject is near coming to a standstill owing to the dead weight of preparations which are required before going further. Until a generation of systematisers shall arise, archaeology can scarcely progress without continual waste of material and loss by duplication of work. Moreover, there is no general reference work, and no notation efficient for recording new discoveries.

Need of a *corpus.*

What is now urgently needed is for some scholars to each take one branch of work, to collect all that is known, especially of dated material ; and then to publish all type examples, showing how the subject varied from century to century, and to attach a system of letters and numbers to every variety, so that any specimen can be denoted merely by its *corpus* number. This should be done at least for all implements of stone and of metal, all pottery, all stone and metal vases, all beads and personal ornaments, jewellery, clothing, domestic utensils, and all motives of design and ornamentation.

With such a definite notation once laid down, it would be possible to record discoveries, and especially groups of objects, rapidly and in a small compass. It would also be possible to compile results of excavations and the contents of museums in simple indices. In order to work systematically in archaeology we ought to be able to look in an index and find at once where, and of what epoch, is every instance of a particular object : say, of a key, type M 27, or of a vase, type D 64. Such indices should be continued by supplements issued every ten or twenty years. At present, if one would ascertain the parallels to a particular form, it is necessary to search through hundreds of volumes and to visit all the museums — a matter of months of work. Progress in archaeology, as an exact science, is practically impossible ; it should be easy and rapid, were all the known material always to be found at once in a *corpus* and indices.

Only one *corpus* has yet been formed, and that is restricted to only one country, one period, and one material — the prehistoric pottery of Egypt (see *Nagada* and *Diospolis Parva*). An outline of the system there followed will serve to show the actual working of a *corpus*, though for each different subject the details will need separate consideration. The whole of this

Example of corpus.

pottery comprises about a thousand varieties. Each class of pottery is denoted by its initial letter ; P for polished, B for black-topped, etc. Each form in a class is numbered, from 1 to 99, and each sub-variety is lettered. Thus R 63 *c* means rough pottery, type 63, variety *c* ; and this completely defines the example. The numbers are not always continuous, but gaps in the series are left where there is much difference between the forms. In this manner it is possible to add new forms without upsetting the system, and new sub-varieties can be brought in by using small letters. The forms are best classified by beginning with the most open and flat dishes, and proceeding to the most closed forms, with narrow necks ending. The point of reaching verticality in the sides is a well-defined middle point.

The practical utility of such a *corpus* is found at once when excavating. Formerly it was needful to keep dozens of broken specimens, which were of no value except for the fact of Utility. being found along with other vases. Now the excavator merely needs to look over the *corpus* of plates, and writes down on the plan of the tomb, say, B 23, P 35 *b*, C 15, F 72, thus the whole record is made, and not a single piece need be kept unless it is a good specimen. How essential such a record is for future progress we shall see below.

The most obvious step now would be to corporate all the pottery of Italy. A *corpus* from Pompeii would be the best starting-point, as being all of one period and well dated ; then a *corpus* of Constantinian forms, a *corpus* of Republican forms, and a *corpus* of each of the prehistoric periods. The early history of the Forum at Rome hangs now upon the safety of little groups of potsherds lying in a shed, yet unclassed and unstudied, and certain to be swept away some day by some one who does not value them. Instead of this we ought to have a *corpus* for reference, and then the contents of each of the archaic wells could be at once denoted and published by the numbers of the types; the historic material would be safe, and could be studied at any future time irrespective of the conservation of the heaps of sherds. Carry this out in Greece, and, instead of piles of pottery lying in the fields or on the terraces of a classical site from the prehistoric town levels, each piece could be noted by its number, and all could be published to make the history of the site accessible. Without a *corpus* such discoveries are but a pathetic destruction of material; with *corpus* notation they would form the basis of a thorough history of the site and of all its changes.

All that is needed to produce a *corpus* from a collection is a month or two of work by a draughts-man, who has an accurate eye for form, working to a uniform scale, and systematising the material conveniently for future reference. Some subjects would require collecting from many sources, but generally all the pottery of one period can be found together in one museum.

We now turn to the second method for archaeo-logical research. This is the synthetical arrangement Successive ages. of the material in the original order. The most obvious arrangement is that by contemporary dating, as by years named in a chronicle or on coins, or by successive reigns of kings. But outside of this method there yet lies the greater part of human history, which can only be reconstructed by some internal evidence of successive periods.

A couple of generations ago there were laid down the main divisions of successive ages of stone, bronze, and iron ; and then the division of the stone age into palaeolithic and neolithic. After that followed the separation of palaeolithic into four main periods in France, more or less applicable to other lands. Further definition was yet found to be necessary, and the neolithic and bronze ages were marked off into many classes, which had to be distinguished by the names of places where they were first found ; and thus we reach a multitude of names, such as Mycenaean, Hallstattian, the period of La Tène, etc. Such a piecemeal plan is well enough for a beginning ; but it is not capable of exact definition, it is cumbersome, and it does not express the relation of one period to another.

Before we can think of subdividing a period into a continuous notation, the first requisite is to be able to place the material into its original order or sequence. Let us suppose some old country mansion, where it has been the habit to close permanently any room in which an owner had died, and leave everything in it undisturbed. If we went through such a series of rooms we could not doubt their order of date if we looked at their contents. The William IV room could not be put to the middle of George III's reign ; the George II room could not be supposed to go between those of James II and Anne. Each room full of furniture

Sequences.

would have some links of style with that of the generation before, and of the generation after it, and no real doubt could exist as to the sequence of the whole series. What is true of a room full of furniture is equally true of a grave full of pottery. If we compare together a series of groups of pottery which are not separated by any long time, there will always be found some relationship between the forms in different groups : one group will be seen to fall between two others if it contains forms to be found in each of the other groups, though these others may have nothing in common together. A fragment of the alphabet, K L M N O P, must fall between H I J K L and O P Q R, and proves their connection.

Thus if each form lasted in use for a uniform length of time the problem would be fairly simple. But it is complicated by the plainer forms lasting far longer in use than the complex or highly decorated forms ; some may go on being made for a thousand years, others may not have been made for even ten years. Hence it is needful to resort to various statistical modes of sorting, which differ in each case. A complete instance of the process is given in *Diospolis Parva*, pp. 4-8.

On the other hand, the sorting of material is greatly helped by any clear series of forms derived one from the other ; especially a series of degradation, and reduction of useful elements to mere ornament. It is well, however, to have a check on one end of a series, by connecting it to known times, so as to prove which way it proceeds.

What notation should be used to express a series

of sequences must vary with conditions. Where we can deal with a larger number—many hundreds—of good graves, each containing plenty of material, then a scale of equal numbers of graves is perhaps the fairest that can be taken. Thus for a scale of sequence dates, for the pottery named above, I adopted 50 numbers, each representing 20 graves.

Sequence dates.

The final result is to express the time-range of each type of pottery and of other objects in the graves in terms of the scale of sequence of the tombs. Thus the date of certain forms may be stated as 33-42 sequence date; 37-70 sequence date; 45-48 sequence date, etc. And when this is once established it is easy to date all further graves by arranging the dates of each object found in a grave, for instance in actual cases :—

Sequence dates.	Sequence dates.
30–36	35–68
32–68	60–69
30–42	68–78
31–34	68–78
Limits 32–34	68

The larger the group the more closely it is dated, by reason of the various forms having a very small common ground of dating.

This system enables us to deal with material which is entirely undated otherwise ; and the larger the quantity of it the more accurate are the results. There is no reason now why prehistoric ages, from which there are groups of remains, should not be

K

dealt with as surely and clearly as the historic ages with recorded dates.

Yet another all-important matter for the systematic archaeology of the future must be here
Conservation.   mentioned, especially as it greatly affects the future schemes of field-work.   The first requirement for systematic work of study is material sufficient to work on.   And to provide this there must be both discovery and conservation. During the last century there has been a gradual growth of archaeological perception ; and in place of only caring for beautiful and striking objects there has arisen some interest in whatever can throw light on the past civilisations.   But unhappily the ideas of conservation have not kept pace with the work of discovery.   The present system of museums is the most serious bar to the progress of archaeology. The building, which is the mere modern shell, of no interest, and often of no beauty, is the master of the collection, which is restrained and crippled by such conditions that its use is impaired and its growth is stopped.   The past is vanishing before our modern changes yearly and daily.   There is ever less and less to preserve.   And everything possible must be garnered before it has entirely vanished.   The present has its most serious duty to history in saving the past for the benefit of the future.

In a museum the collection is the essential ; the building is the mere accident of the surroundings of
Buildings.   the collection, and it should completely conform to all the requirements.   Yet can it be believed that, even in the last year or two, enormous national museums—as at Cairo and

Brussels—have been built without the smallest regard
to the collection, or the opinions of the curators?
The result at Cairo is the most deplorable sacrifice
of the art and history of a great country to the
follies and childish vanity of an incompetent and
unsympathetic architect. We will not stay to detail
the entire unsuitability of that building in style,
form, size, and lighting; the constructive questions
of what is needed for a proper museum are our
subject.

After the common purpose of all buildings—
security from man and nature—the first requirements in a museum are lighting and
grouping. Whatever interferes with
these is a detriment which should be avoided or
removed. Lighting must be (1) direct, not from
reflection by walls; (2) full, but not dazzling; (3)
in exactly the right direction. Of all the precious
statues of antiquity there is not one that has had a
tenth of its value spent on the best lighting possible.
Most are in hopelessly bad positions, as the
Aphrodite of Melos in a weak, diffused, sidelight;
and none have the simplest blinds to change the
direction of the light, so as to study the surface in
varying lighting. To know what a figure requires,
only take a fine statuette in the hand, and try what
can be made of it by the variation of direction,
obliquity, and amount of lighting. Then see how
hopeless it is to know a statue in one fixed lighting,
even if that be suitable. The only person competent
to arrange the lighting of objects, and especially
statuary, is a successful photographer who has well
practised the lighting of portable figures. An

Lighting.

almost vertical light is essential for all human figures in the round or flat ; but it needs most delicate adjustment to bring out the more important modelling, and many different directions of light to shew all that there is in the work. What is true of statuary is true in a lesser degree of every other object. No other qualities can possibly atone for defects of lighting in a museum. No building with a bad light can be called properly a museum ; it may be an architect's triumph, a civic ornament, a costly patchwork, a marvel of folly, but a museum it is not, if it is unfit for the first requirements of a collection.

The second great requirement, that of grouping, includes the intelligent display of objects so as to shew their relation to each other in development, their connection as found together, the preservation of the whole of the material that should be preserved, and its comparison by means of casts.

Grouping.

The relation of objects in development requires free space in a museum, and the absence of any pinching consideration of how to utilise every square foot. Their connection as found together in tombs and groups also requires free space, more than is yet to be had in any English museum. The preservation of the whole of the needful material is still more utterly beyond the limits of any of the present museums. Every year a great deal of entirely irreplaceable material is thrown away, or neglected on the spot, because there is no hope whatever of preserving it. In the British Museum space costs several pounds a square foot, and only objects of great value can be reasonably preserved there. We are driven, then, to the conclusion that the progress of archaeology and the preservation of the past, as it comes into our hands year by year, is essentially a question of free space. And that is practically entirely a question of cheap space. To refuse to preserve anything that is not worth some pounds per square foot, is the death of archaeology; and yet such are the necessary conditions in our present museums, however much we may expand them in their costly conditions. If we once think of what the condition of affairs will be fifty years hence, when many periods and places will be exhausted, and yet nothing but showy objects are preserved, we see that the future knowledge of archaeology is help-lessly bound up in the question of our immediate expansion of conservation.

We see then how absolutely necessary for archae-ology and ethnology it is to have a National Repository, where the cost of space shall never be detrimental to the collection. National Repository. I need not enter on the details of how such a repository could be carried out, as I have fully discussed them at the British Association, and the Society of Arts (see *Jour. S. A.* No. 2, 478, price 6d.); but an outline of the conditions and cost will shew the practicability of the proposal. All objects of value to a thief should be kept in the strong custody of city museums; but the great majority of speci-mens that should be preserved are too bulky or too unsaleable to be stolen, beside casts which no one would steal, and such do not, therefore, need more than general supervision. A square mile of land, within an hour's journey from London, should be secured ; and built over with uniform plain brickwork and cement galleries, at the rate of 20,000 square feet a year, so providing 8 miles of galleries 50 feet wide in a century, with room yet for several centuries of expansion at the same rate. A staff of about 30 persons would suffice to arrange the new material at this rate ; and having abundant space, no time would be wasted by frequent shifting of old material. Everything should be photographically registered as it came in. Glass should be placed over all objects which can deteriorate ; but the amount of dirt would be a minimum in the country, and with the air-supply filtered from dust.

The total cost of land, building, materials, and staff would be covered by a budget of £10,000 a year. And this is the normal *increase* of the British Museum budget every four years. Hence if the British Museum were to find room by clearing out objects which are not liable to be stolen, for a few years, and placing them in the Repository, the cost of the Repository would be paid for to all time. A mere retardation of growth of the British Museum for five or ten years would entirely make up for the cost of the Repository twenty times its size. That this provision is perfectly practicable is not denied ; that it would be far cheaper than continued expansion in highly expensive conditions is certain ; and that it is essential for the growth of archaeology and ethnology is sadly obvious. Let us hope that if we are too hide-bound in England to grasp the new conditions of research, that at least in America some one will provide such a storehouse for all time ;

where some day the history of the world may be studied, when we have hopelessly lost the chance of preserving what might at present be had for the asking. If we are to make up our minds to ignore and lose what is now being lost and destroyed every year owing to our ignorance and blindness, we must look to the New World to rescue from our misuse the material we now throw away, and so preserve the history of mankind.

CHAPTER XII

ARCHAEOLOGICAL EVIDENCE

THE nature of proof is more complex than it seems to be at first sight. True enough, all proof is merely

Nature of proof. a matter of common sense ; it does not appeal to any different faculty. And though a proof may follow as simply as possible from the facts, yet it cannot be understood by one who is not familiar with the facts to begin with. Trigonometry is the most obvious common sense to any one familiar with the formulae ; and the formulae themselves are only common sense to any one who takes the trouble to argue them through. Yet, for all that, trigonometry is not obvious to the ignorant. In the same way the evidences about the past of man are simple and clear when the facts and methods from which they are deduced are already known. Yet it requires a good familiarity with the material before the conclusions can be felt to be self-evident results.

To follow clearly what evidence and proof means, it is best to refer to a class of evidence which is

Legal evidence. most familiar to the reader. What is commonly called *legal evidence* is the best-known example, as it is met every day in law

136

cases and police reports. Evidence is based on the
same principles, in whatever subject it may be;
there is not one logic for the present, and a different
logic for the past. But the kind of evidence, the
exactitude, the certainty, which is considered enough
to determine a property or a life, is rightly looked
on as conclusive for all reasonable purposes. The
laws of such evidence have been threshed over for
generations past; and it is well known what kind of
proofs may be relied upon, and what are dubious. If
we then compare this class of evidence with that which
we accept in studying the past history of man, we shall
see more clearly what kinds of proof are admissible,
and how far it is reasonable to depend upon our results.

In examining legal evidence we see that it all
falls under one of four heads—(1) witnesses, (2)
material objects, (3) exhaustion, and (4) probabilities.
These four kinds of evidence are of very different
values; any one of them may be stronger than the
others in a given case, and each kind has its own
special weakness.

1. *Witnesses* provide the most clear and connected proof, and the least liable to misunderstanding; but yet a proof which is entirely dependent on
veracity, on intelligence, on absence of prejudice, and
on clear memory, and is hence the least dependable
kind of evidence in some cases.

2. *Material facts*, which may be very conclusive;
such as A's footprint in B's garden, or A's chisel
left in B's house, at a burglary. If the fact is certain,
the conclusion is proved; but the danger lies in
misunderstanding the fact.

3. *Exhaustion*, which may prove A guilty because

no one else could have done the deed ; as when A
and B are seen in a railway carriage at one station,
and at the next stoppage B is found murdered and
A leaves the carriage.   There may be not a trace of
other evidence, but this is enough.

4. *Probability*, as when A is last seen with B, and
B proceeds to deal with the property of murdered A.
This kind of evidence is enough to hang a man, solely
from presumption.

Now let us look at these kinds of evidence about
the past of man.

1. *Witnesses*, the documents, which give a clear
and connected statement.   They may be either
primary, as a stone inscription or an
autograph letter ; or secondary, as compiled histories or subsequent copies.   No other kind
of evidence is so easy to follow ; yet this is a proof
in which we are entirely at the mercy of the pre-
judices, the ill-will, the frauds, and the blunders of
others, and it is hence the least dependable kind of
evidence in some cases.   The speeches of Thucydides,
the bias of Suetonius, the wonders of Livy, the
romances of William of Malmesbury, and the forgery
called Richard of Cirencester, each plunge us deeper
and deeper into the doubtfulness of written documents ; to say nothing of the casket letters or Ossian.

2. *Material facts*, when rightly understood, are
the most conclusive evidence.   They may be in a
single object, as a palaeolithic flint re-
chipped over and over in later ages ; or
a foreign ornament used on an object of dated style,
as a Maori tatued head in a daguerreotype would
prove the tatuing to be known between 1840 and

1860 ; or a restruck coin with one type over another, as Barchocheb over Hadrian ; or an added inscription, so familiar on Egyptian statues. Or the evidence may consist in a collocation of objects, such as a group of things found together in a tomb ; or the superposition of strata of ruins in a town. In the case of a single object there are few possibilities of misunderstanding the evidence ; but in strata or tomb-groups there is a chance of older things being reused. Such chances of error are, however, extinguished by the recurrence of instances ; and the finding of certain things together in several cases under different circumstances is one of the strongest kinds of evidence, such, for instance, as the name of Amenhotep III often found with the Mykenaean pottery, both in Greece and in Egypt.

3. *Exhaustion* may prove a point ; as, for instance, the Iconoclasts in Greece or Reformers and Puritans in England were the only destroyers of images and pictures, or Akhenaten was the only man who erased the name of Amen. Such destructions therefore are evidence of the age and the man.

Exhaustion.

4. *Probabilities*, as, for instance, the fact that the Saxons erased the Romano-Britons, makes it probable that Silchester, Uriconium, and other late Roman towns which were burnt, were destroyed by the Saxons.

Probabilities.

We see thus that each kind of proof which is accepted legally is also used archaeologically, and is subject to much the same failings. Legal evidence may fail by mistaking the nature of the facts, such as that some rabbit's blood on a knife is human blood ; so may archaeology mistake by ignorance, as when the Mykenaean treasure was called Byzantine.

Or legal evidence may fail by wrong inferences from facts, such as that some human blood on a knife is due to a murder, while it has come from the owner's finger. So archaeology erred from a wrong inference in calling the treasure of Troy " the treasure of Priam."

Or legal evidence may fail owing to mere prejudice, thus ignoring the truth. So archaeology has suffered from the prejudice that nothing in Greece can be older than the VIIIth century B.C.

It is supposed sometimes, by those unfamiliar with the subject, that archaeological evidence is so doubtful or so slight that it cannot be

Legal proof.

relied upon, and is not to be compared with the certainties of legal proof. Let us see then what legal proof is in important cases. In one case a will was lost, and the mere memory of its contents, stated by a survivor who had assisted in writing it, was accepted as sufficient proof of what had been in it, and the property was distributed accordingly. In another case property was left by A to B, or failing B to C ; B also made a will leaving it to D. A and B were killed together in an accident, and the slightest observation of which moved last, determined whether C or D had the property. Again, there are innumerable cases of setting a will aside because of the testator not being of a sound mind for disposing of property ; and various assertions of irrelevant facts by various interested parties are held to reveal the true mental capacity of a person to a judge and jury. In a murder trial the question of whether one or both of the assailants were guilty was held proved by the deceased having been tied by two different forms of knots. In another trial the mere presumption due to concealing a body and dealing with the property of a murdered person was enough to hang a man. Such are some of the evidences which are held good in law to settle questions of life and property.

Happily archaeology is relieved from the terrible dilemma of being bound to come to a conclusion at once, as the law has to do. Questions can be left pending, and it is not peremptorily needful to act one way or another. An open mind can be kept on difficult and obscure points ; and a matter can be discussed in fresh lights, without keeping a prisoner standing in the dock the whole time. Legal conclusions are often wrong ; though, as the law can do no wrong, a free pardon is all the sufferer gets when his innocence is proved. But if legal proofs, arguments, and conclusions were kept freely open to revision for years ; if they were printed in every textbook for beginners ; if all students were encouraged to find fresh evidence, and to upset what was laid down, and if the high-road to position lay in reversing the decisions of past authorities, it seems only too likely that there would be a greater wreckage of bad cases and bad law than there now is of bad archaeology.

For an example of the nature of archaeological evidence it will be best to study the connections of Egypt with early Europe. This subject Egypt and is not only a fascinating one historically, Europe. but it includes a great variety of different kinds of evidence,—from paintings, from groups found in tombs, from remains of palaces, from objects exactly dated by royal names, from objects dated by their nature and style ; and evidence which is of various degrees of certainty.   Moreover this evidence has been more actively and continually attacked than any other class of discoveries of late years, and hence the most that can be argued against it is well known.

Until 1883 nothing was known of the Greeks in Egypt before the Ptolemaic age ; the accounts of In XXVIth Herodotus about the Greek mercenaries, Dynasty. and their connection with the XXVIth Dynasty, stood solely as a literary statement, without a scrap of tangible evidence.   At the close of that year I bought an archaic Greek statuette in Cairo (Fig. 56) ; and on enquiring about the source of it, I heard of Nebireh, and hunted out the site in the Western Delta.   There I found the ground covered with archaic Greek pottery dating throughout the XXVIth Dynasty, and it was evident that a great Greek city had existed there.   Next year, at the close of 1884, I began exploring it, and found on the first day there, a decree of the people of Nau-kratis.   Here then the evidence of Greek occupation depended upon the presence of thousands of pieces of Greek pottery and sculpture ; and to imagine that these had all been imported by Egyptians was beyond any possible supposition.   A town containing almost entirely Greek remains, and with only clumsy imitations of Egyptian subjects, was certainly occu-pied by Greeks.   And as there is no instance or probability of Greeks having imported great quantities of vases made in earlier times, this place contained good evidence for Greeks having lived there from the VIIth century B.C. As such it was generally accepted; but the dedication by the Naukratites was withheld from the public for six months by over-cautious authorities, for fear that something else might contradict it. This is a case where what was undoubtedly good evidence should rather have been stated at once, with a reservation that it was very improbable that the stone had been brought from another site, or dedicated anywhere except in Naukratis. The evidence of the pottery shewed that Naukratis dated from the middle of the VIIth century; and this agrees with the statement by Athenaeus that a statue was dedicated there in the 23rd Olympiad, 688 B.C.

In the next season, the spring of 1886, I went down to Defeneh, and there found a great mass of Greek pottery of the same period as that of Naukratis. Here again, then, the Greeks had inhabited the site; and the evidence was clear that this was a great camp of Greek mercenaries. The modern name Defeneh so closely agrees to the ancient Daphnae that no one hesitated to accept their equivalence. Here the identification rests, then, not on a contemporary inscription, but on a modern Arabic name.

Important evidence about the manufactures of these places is given by the pottery. Although the two sites were occupied at the same period by Ionian Greeks, yet the bulk of the pottery on one site differs from that on the other. The conclusion is that probably it was made locally by Greek potters, and not brought by traders from Greek towns, as trade would probably have imported from the same sources to both sites. The evidence here is from the difference of classes.

Another conclusion is drawn from the few varieties of painted pottery which are found in common at both sites. From the levels at which they were found at Naukratis these varieties were dated at various years between 610 and 550 B.C.; and such varieties were found together in a chamber at Defeneh with jar sealings bearing royal names of Psamtek II and Aahmes, and therefore dated between 595 and 565 B.C., as the Greeks were removed from the camp in the latter year. The evidence here is from the collocation of objects; those dated by the levels at which other things were found at Naukratis agreeing with those dated by mixture with Egyptian sealings at Defeneh.

We now turn to the great group of dating of the XVIIIth-XXth Dynasties; and as the nature of XVIIIth Dynasty the evidence is our present considera-paintings. tion we shall classify it according to the kind of source of the evidence. The most certain dating is that of offerings painted on the walls of tombs, as it is always agreed that such represent objects which were in current use when the tomb was decorated; they therefore are not older than the tomb, nor can the paintings have been added later. Of this class are the paintings of vases in the tomb of Rekhmara, under Tahutmes III in the XVIIIth Dynasty; these vases are shewn as being brought in by the Kefti foreigners, and strongly resemble the vases found in Cyprus, Mykenae, and other Greek sites. Here the con-

THE GREEKS IN EGYPT.

Fig. 56. Warrior, in alabaster.
Naukratis, XXVI Dyn.

Fig. 57. Graeco-Egyptian vases.
Abydos, XVIII Dyn.

nection of Egypt in the XVIIIth Dynasty with people
who made such vases is certain ; but the vases might
be older than the scene, or such vases might continue
to be made to a later time, hence the connection
with any given epoch on Greek soil is only a strong
probability but not absolute. Another dated painting is that of stirrup vases (to use a more convenient
word than " pseud-amphorae," " false-necked vases,"
or " *bügel kanne* ") among the offerings in the paintings on the tomb of Ramessu III of the XXth
Dynasty. That such forms were familiar at that
date is absolute ; but they might be older vases
preserved in the Royal Treasury, or might be
imitations by Egyptians of older foreign forms, like
English repetition of Chinese patterns.

The next class of evidence is that of objects
which have been placed in such conditions that they
cannot have been disturbed after a given
date. This evidence is given by several
deposits of groups of vases, clothing, etc., which
were burnt in pits sunk in the floors of houses, and
then earthed over. Such groups cannot possibly
have been disturbed later on to insert objects, as the
charcoal and ashes are undisturbed, and the foreign
objects are likewise burnt. Hence the evidence of
the Egyptian objects if clearly dated must carry the
foreign objects to the same date. Several such
groups have been found at Gurob. In one were
many Egyptian objects all agreeing well to the date
of Amenhotep III, as fixed by a glazed pottery
kohl tube ; in another a group agreeing with the
date of Tutankhamen, which was shewn by some
fragile pendants which could not have long survived

Burnt groups.

L

in use ; another group agrees to the age of Ramessu
II, who is named on a pendant of glazed ware ; and
a fourth group agrees to the rougher style of Sety
II, which is dated by a dish with his name.   The
character of the Egyptian objects thus points to
each of these dated objects being contemporary
with the rest of their group, and therefore truly
dating the group.   Now in these groups were first,
five well-made globular stirrup vases (see Fig. 59) ;
second, pieces of several stirrup vases of a later
form ; third, the neck of a later and coarser
stirrup vase ; and fourth, two much later coarse
and unpainted stirrup vases.   Here the changes in
the character of the vases agree with the relative
dates given by the Egyptian objects.   The stirrup
vases might be all older than the Egyptian dates,
but that is very improbable by the regular degradation of them according with the dates; and the groups
cannot be later than the dated objects as they agree
well with the date of such Egyptian things fixed
in other cases.   It is then extremely improbable
that the stirrup vases should not belong to the
periods of the Egyptian kings whose names are
found with them.   Variation in either direction is
prohibited by these limitations.

We may add that there are two other burnt groups
without kings' names, and the connection of stirrup
vases with Egyptian objects in these agrees well
with the connection shewn by the other groups.
Another such grouping was in a burial in open
ground at Abydos ; there several examples of
Graeco-Egyptian ware (Fig. 57), two figures and a
ring vase with pomegranates and lotus flowers, were

found with Egyptian pottery and beads of the XVIIIth Dynasty.

A somewhat similar grouping is afforded by the rubbish mounds of the palace of Akhenaten at Tell el Amarna. There the palace was Rubbish mounds. entirely deserted after the reign of his successor, about 1360 B.C., and the town ruined finally by Horemheb, 1330 B.C. It seems then impossible to suppose anything later being mixed up with the rubbish heaps, which contained nearly a hundred dated objects, none later than 1360 B.C. The supposition has even been suggested that some unknown people, who left no other traces, have at some later time come laden with hundreds of potsherds, and dug over the rubbish mounds to mix them together. Such are the wild fancies which must be resorted to if the evidence is to be upset. The rubbish mounds consist of some thousands of tons of potsherds and dust; and among these, entirely mixed with them, were found nearly a hundred rings and objects of Akhenaten and his successor, and over 1300 pieces of Aegean pottery, representing probably 800 vases. The palace, which was deserted after 1360 B.C., also contained several pieces of the same pottery. Here the great quantity of the material of all kinds precludes all the suppositions that might be made about isolated specimens. The mounds are too large for later material to be mixed with them; the dated objects are too many to be accidental, or to have been older than the mounds; and the Aegean vases are too many to have been preserved from earlier times. The whole conditions prove that all the objects were in common use contemporaneously.

A somewhat less certain dating is given by remains found in houses. At the palace of Akhenaten the definite date of its ruin fairly shews the Aegean pottery in it to be contemporary with his generation. In a house at Gurob, Aegean pottery was found with wood-carving of the XIXth Dynasty and a ring of the late XVIIIth Dynasty, and also under the walls of a house which was built at the close of the XVIIIth Dynasty. These are not precise datings, and are open to claims that the houses were later than the evidence shews; but such connections give a strong presumption.

Houses.

Similar, but converse, evidence is given from the Greek side. At Mykenae was found a figure of a monkey in violet glaze (No. 4573 Athens); this is of Egyptian work and bears the name of Amenhotep II. A piece of glaze found in a building by the lion gate has the name of Amenhotep III. A scarab of Thyi, his queen, was found in the palace of Mykenae. And three large jars of drab-coloured Egyptian pottery (4569 Athens), such as is quite unknown from Greek sources, were also found at Mykenae. Now these examples prove the import of Egyptian things of the XVIIIth and XIXth Dynasties before the fall of Mykenae; they do not give an exact dating as their time-connection on the Greek side is unstated, and they might belong to any part of the history of the town. But their agreement in age gives a strong presumption that the latter half of the XVIIIth

Dynasty was contemporary with some part of the flourishing period of foreign trade at Mykenae.

At this point we should notice an assertion often made, that Egyptian objects, especially scarabs, often bore the names of kings who were earlier than the date of the manufacture. This Scarabs. is sometimes the case, and on this ground it has been attempted to discredit all evidence about scarabs. Now an exactly similar case occurs in Roman coinage, where at eight different periods restorations of coins of earlier emperors took place, no less than twenty emperors being thus commemorated. Yet no one has impugned the evidence of Roman coins in dating an excavation, on the ground that as some were restored therefore none are of certain value. Similarly seven kings restored the scarabs of earlier times, twelve different kings being thus commemorated ; but that is no reason for discrediting the age of the remaining ninety-nine scarabs out of every hundred. The restorations, say of the XIIth Dynasty kings by Tahutmes III, are as obvious as the restorations of earlier emperors by Gallienus. No doubt to a person ignorant of coins the subject would seem uncertain and confused ; but then scientific evidence is not expected to appeal to those who are ignorant of the subject, whether it be coins or scarabs. We must then credit the evidence of scarabs for dating, although there are some restored in a different style, and although some case might be found where a scarab had been reused at a much later date than that of its manufacture. Such exceptions are certainly not one per cent of the whole, and cannot therefore be invoked to explain away the whole of the instances.

The largest class of evidence is that from collocation in tombs. The weak points of this are (1)

Tombs in
Egypt.

reuse of tombs so that primary and secondary interments may be mixed ; this should be obvious in any properly conducted excavation, and cannot be brought in as an hypothesis unless some mixture of date can be otherwise proved : (2) the tomb contents being older than the dated object, and so brought to too low a date, which is very unlikely, as a whole group of things would not be preserved for long together : (3) the dated object being older than the tomb, which is practically the only danger. A few rare examples have been seen of older objects being reburied, but so rarely that only a very small proportion of cases could be thus explained. The great majority of things in hand at any one time belong to within a generation or two. In our own time, although we treasure older things more than did the people of any past age, yet not one per cent of what we have is over a hundred years old. In late Roman coinage the waste was such that in a hundred years only an eighth survived in use, and in half a century more only a twenty-fifth remained. It is very rarely that beads or pendants of very different ages are mixed in ancient necklaces, or that scarabs of reigns far apart are buried together. I do not remember a mixture of more than two contiguous reigns in any group of scarabs that I have found. Hence this possibility of an older object being reused may occur rarely, but cannot be called upon in the whole of the cases, or even for any perceptible proportion of them. In certainly nine cases out of ten we must expect that a dated object was buried within less than two or three generations from its original period.

The tomb groups containing Aegean pottery are, it so happens, not so well dated as the burnt groups; and are therefore inferior to the burnt groups, both on this account, as well as by the greater possibility of mixture. The Maket tomb at Kahun is the principal example. The dated objects in that are of Tahutmes II and III; and though at first I supposed it to be of later age on the strength of some beads not then known before the XIXth or XXth Dynasty, yet as such beads were afterwards found in a deposit of Tahutmes III at Koptos, there is no reason for questioning that the whole is of his age. Also the experience of the past dozen years has shewn that such a date agrees well to all the other objects in the tomb. The absence of blue painted pottery does not imply a date after the disuse of it in the XXth Dynasty, but before that style came into use in the middle of the XVIIIth Dynasty. In this tomb was a fine Aegean vase (Fig. 58) with ivy-spray pattern, which is thus dated to about 1500 B.C. The burials were quite undisturbed and therefore the vase cannot belong to a later date, but might possibly be earlier.

Other examples have not this precise dating. At Kahun a burial in the open ground, and undisturbed, had scarabs and objects of the style of the middle or end of the XVIIIth Dynasty, with a stirrup vase from the Aegean (*Kahun*, p. 32). The undisturbed tomb at Gurob containing the beautiful wooden statuette of Res, certainly of the XVIIIth Dynasty, had in an opposite chamber a stirrup vase, which must have been buried at the same period. Another burial at Gurob had a piece of a stirrup vase with beads exactly like those of Ramessu II. And at Naqada a tomb which by the style of the painting, must have belonged to the beginning or middle of the XVIIIth Dynasty, had been so entirely plundered that the only object left was a fine globular stirrup vase. In these cases

FIG. 58.—Aegean vase of Tahutmes III. Maket tomb. 1 : 3.

there is no exact dating, but a consensus of style in each case of the XVIIIth or early XIXth Dynasty ; and the connection of the Aegean pottery with it is in some cases absolute and in others only presumptive. The argument for date of the pottery rests then in these cases on the uniformity of the period connected with it, and the absence of any discrepant dating.

Now this argument is greatly reinforced if we can shew that the same connection of period exists on Tombs in the other side. At Ialysos in Rhodes a Greece. tomb with Aegean pottery contained a scarab of Amenhotep III. At Mykenae, grave No. 49 contained also glazed ware of Amenhotep III. At Enkomi in Cyprus in grave 93 a scarab of Queen Thyi was found with Aegean pottery. And from the same cemetery comes a metal ring of her son Amenhotep IV. These cases therefore connect one period of the Aegean remains with the Egyptian

reigns from 1414 to 1365 B.C.   If on one hand it
might be supposed that the single Greek objects in
Egyptian tombs were older than the time of their
burial, here on the other hand the possibility is
reversed, and the single Egyptian objects in Greece
could only be older and not later than the group
with which they were buried.   As on both sides the
dating is the same—the latter part of the XVIIIth
Dynasty—it shows that in both countries the groups
contained objects of contemporary date.   If we were
to further refine on the question, and enquire whether
the differences of date of the reigns in Egypt correspond to equal differences in Greece, we are met by
the lack of all relative dating yet assignable to the
Greek tombs ; on that side we have only a vague
statement of " Mykenaean period," or some such
generality ; and it is therefore only that period in
general that we can assign to the XVIIIth-XIXth
Dynasty in Egypt.

We may, however, see a little further into detail
on the Egyptian side by observing how the stirrup
vases vary in form and work.   At Naqada,   Variation
probably under Tahutmes III, was a   with date.
globular form, with simple broad bands, and dull
face.   At Gurob under Amenhotep III the vases
have more broad bands and a polished face (Fig. 59).
Under Tutankhamen there were fine lines appearing
between the bands.   Under Ramessu II the form is
coarser.   And under Sety II is only a coarse unpainted imitation.   Lastly, under Ramessu VI at
Tell el Yehudiyeh were some rude debased copies.
Here the relative style of the vases agrees with the
varying date of the objects found with each ; and

hence we are justified in not only placing one general period in Greece as contemporary with another period in Egypt, but also in connecting the varied forms with the reigns which are named with them. The evidence which we gain from the mere general admixture, without any proof of the objects originating

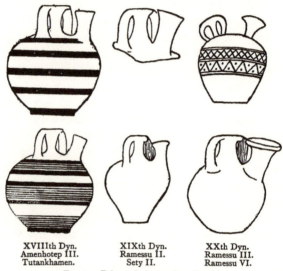

| XVIIIth Dyn. Amenhotep III. Tutankhamen. | XIXth Dyn. Ramessu II. Sety II. | XXth Dyn. Ramessu III. Ramessu VI. |

Fig. 59.—False-necked vases from Egypt.

in the generation by which they were buried, is here further carried on into evidence for the exact age of each type by the sequence of style agreeing to the sequence of the dated objects.

We now turn to a question of style alone. In grave 93 at Enkomi was found a gold collar of Egyptian work with nine different patterns in it; of these, eight are well known as designs of the time of Amenhotep IV, and the ninth

Style.

is a variant of such.   As these designs are not known in such forms at a century later or earlier, this collar cannot have been made far from 1400 B.C.; and as it is of slight and tender fabric it cannot have long been in use.   Hence the date of its burial and of the tomb must be in the fourteenth century B.C. Of other examples of style, which may be quoted as important, is a great group of blue glazed ware of the same form, colour, and designs, as the vases of Ramessu II, but found in grave 66 at Enkomi; a gold pin, with a hole in the middle, of the XVIIIth-XIXth Dynasty found at Gurob, like one from grave 66 at Enkomi; a group of bronze vases with lotus handles found in the Idaean cave in Crete, exactly of the fabric of those of the XVIIIth-XIXth Dynasty; a figure of a swimming girl holding a dish, carved in bone, from the Idaean cave, a favourite design in the XVIIIth Dynasty; and some other instances of similar style, ornament, and processes, which need hardly reinforce the general argument.

To recapitulate the evidences of the XVIIIth-XXth Dynasty :—   Recapitulation.

    Evidence of paintings.   Tombs of Rekhmara and Ramessu III.

      Result.   Aegean objects possibly older than the paintings.

    Evidence of burnt groups.   Four, from Amenhotep III to Sety II.

      Result.   Aegean pottery possibly older than the groups.

    Evidence of rubbish heaps.   Tell el Amarna.

      Result.   Aegean pottery certainly contemporary with Amenhotep IV.

Evidence of houses.   Tell el Amarna, Gurob,
Mykenae.

Result.   Aegean pottery probably of XVIIIth
Dynasty.   Greek houses probably of XVIIIth
Dynasty.

Evidence of tombs.   Maket tomb ; tombs at
Gurob, Mykenae, and Enkomi.

Result.   Aegean pottery possibly older than
Tahutmes III ; probably of XVIIIth-XIXth
Dynasty or possibly older ; Greek tombs of
XVIIIth Dynasty, or possibly later.

Evidence of style.   Gold collar.   Idaean vases and
carving.

Result.   Importations to Greece of XVIIIth
Dynasty, and perhaps XIXth ; copy of
XVIIIth Dynasty design, possibly later.

The possible deviations from the probable results
are thus seen to balance one another, some leaving
the limit only open to earlier times and some only
to later times, so that change cannot be accepted in
either direction.

We now go back to an earlier stage in the
history, that of the XIIth Dynasty.   Some ten years
XIIth Dynasty, ago the stage which we have already
Kahun.   discussed was the " fighting frontier " of
the subject ; five years ago the XIIth Dynasty was
the fighting frontier ; now this is almost pacified, and
the struggle against prepossessions is carried back to
the still earlier periods.

The view back to the XIIth Dynasty was first
opened out in excavating the rubbish mounds of the
town of Kahun.   This town was entirely built at
one time for the workmen employed on the pyramid

of Usertesen II, this then is the starting date. While the houses were fully occupied a large rubbish mound was accumulated outside of the walls. When the official work of building ceased at the finishing of the pyramid, we may conclude that the town began to dwindle, as I found many of the houses and streets had been used as rubbish holes for waste of the XIIth Dynasty. Therefore the less convenient and accessible rubbish heap outside of the walls is probably entirely of the reign of Usertesen II. As it does not contain any Egyptian material that could be dated later than that, the evidence of the shrinkage of the town should be accepted as giving a probable limit to the age of the outer heaps.

In these heaps the great bulk was of regular Egyptian pottery of the XIIth Dynasty, filling up a depth of 6 or 8 feet in parts, and therefore very unlikely to become mixed with later objects dropped by accident. Now with this pottery thus certified as to its age, were found pieces of several kinds hitherto entirely unknown. Black ware decorated with white spiral lines, and with yellow and red lines and circles of dots, red pottery with white returning spirals, and with painting in red, white, and green. The style was obviously of the Aegean family, so much so that even the best authorities asserted that these were pieces of Naukratite pottery of the XXVIth Dynasty and shut their eyes to the great difference of fabric and material. For some years I protested that the evidence of finding was absolute for the XIIth Dynasty date, and that no such pottery was known at a later date to which this could be compared. But some general resemblance to the style of the XXVIth Dynasty was allowed to calm the archaeological conscience of my friends into ignoring all the positive evidence. No such pottery was known on Greek soil at an early date ; therefore none existed ; therefore this could not be of that date. This argument is still in full favour for other and earlier periods. But a shock of surprise came when delicate black pottery with white painting and red was found at Kamares in Crete, and published by Mr. Myres in 1895 ; and later the same style of pottery was so largely found that Messrs. Hogarth and Welch write in 1901 that "so far from that ware being a rarity, it is to be looked for in Crete wherever any strata of remains underlie the Mykenaean. It occurred in our digging at Knossos at all points at which the early town was probed to the rock " (*J.H.S.* xxi. 78). The pre-Mykenaean period is now before us and is found to agree entirely with the dating already reached on unimpeachable grounds at Kahun. That we may recognise connections between Greece and Egypt in the XIIth Dynasty is now orthodox, and we may proceed to see what further evidence appears for this dating.

At Knossos was found a portion of an Egyptian seated figure in diorite bearing an inscription of XIIth Dynasty, Ab-nub-mes-uazet-user, which from the Crete. style is probably of the XIIth Dynasty.

At Praesos were found several globular beads of carnelian and of amethyst such as are well known in the XIIth Dynasty, and the latter material is not found dated to a later period in Egypt.

At Knossos was found a globular alabaster vase of the regular type of the XIIth Dynasty ; and also the alabaster vase lid of King Khyan, whose date is unfortunately not fixed on the Egyptian side, but who is probably of the XVIth Dynasty, though perhaps of the XIth.

The long period now known in Greece before the civilization which is dated to the XVIIIth Dynasty compels such a presumption of connection with far earlier periods, and the connection is so well shewn by the Kamares ware, that the evidence for the XIIth Dynasty relationship scarcely needs further support. It depends on identity of style of highly decorated pottery, and of beads; and the transport of two pieces of Egyptian work.

Another connection of this age is shewn by the "pan-grave" pottery found in Egypt. This class of shallow circular graves is dated to the close of the XIIth Dynasty by several Pan graves. discoveries of worn and damaged objects of the XIIth Dynasty in the graves, without anything that could be fixed to a later date. In these graves is a large class of non-Egyptian pottery; some of it black and red, highly polished; others, rude thick pottery with incised patterns. The similarity of the black and red to the style of the prehistoric pottery of Egypt is obvious; it is a later branch of the same fabric. And when we consider from what other land that may have come into Egypt, we naturally look to the similar forms found in the Celtic pottery of Southern Spain by Bonsor (Fig. 60), as indicating that it belongs to the western Libyan culture. Again, the rough incised pottery is of the same Celtic family found in Spain, showing a western source. The suggestion lately put forward that these may have come into Egypt from the East is wholly baseless. It is in Spain and the allied Celtic pottery of Europe that we find the types which were brought into Egypt by the rude invaders at the close of the XIIth Dynasty. So that a connection of the western barbaric culture of the bronze age with the close of the XIIth Dynasty must be concluded, from the evidence of similar pottery in-

Central Europe.
Yorkshire.
(*J. Anth. Inst.*
xxxii., pl. xxvii.)

South Spain.
(*Rev. Arch.*
xxxv. 121-2.)

Diospolis, Egypt.
(*Diospolis,*
xxxviii., xl.)

Fig. 60.—Celtic and pan-grave pottery and ornament.

truded into Egypt, and associated in graves with the objects of that age.

It is probably then to the same invaders that we should look for the source of the black incised ware (Fig. 61) with patterns filled with white, and of characteristically western—Italic or Greek—forms, which is found in Kahun in the XIIth Dynasty, and in burials at Khataaneh of the XIIIth Dynasty. It is the latest stage of a class of imported pottery which recurs at intervals from the early prehistoric age onwards. A piece of this pottery was found in one of the "pan graves," thus linking it with the

EARLIEST. TROY.

NEOLITHIC. BOSNIA.

PREHISTORIC. EGYPT.

I DYN.

III DYN. EGYPT.

XII DYN. EGYPT.

Fig. 61.—Black incised pottery, with white filling.

M

other foreign pottery brought in at that period. It
has been found at Hissarlik in the lowest levels, in
Bosnia at Butmir, and of prehistoric to XIIIth
Dynasty age in Egypt.

On going back another stage to the Old Kingdom,
of the IVth to VIth Dynasties, we still find links
VIth to IIIrd between Egypt and the West. In the
Dynasties.   VIth dynasty is found a class of non-
Egyptian buttons (Fig. 62) with devices, which in

Fig. 62.—Buttons of ivory, carnelian, glazed steatite, etc. VIIth Dyn.
The upper row with misapplied Egyptian designs.
The lower row with entirely un-Egyptian designs. 2 : 3.

some cases may have been used as seals ; more
than a hundred of these are now known, and in no
case are they of Egyptian fabric, as when an
Egyptian subject was copied it was always in a
mistaken manner. Now a close parallel to many of
the designs is found on Cretan engraved stones, and
it is therefore to that civilisation that we must look
for the source of a considerable foreign importation,
which probably accompanied a movement of population at the overthrow of the civilisation of the Old

Kingdom. The actual incomers may have passed by sea from the islands, or by land along Africa.

On turning to Crete we see in the noble lamp with lotus capital found at Knossos, a type which cannot have been derived from anything that we know of the XIIth Dynasty in Egypt. The free buds around the band had long since become lost at that time; and even in the Vth Dynasty on the Abusir capital they are less distinct. A form belonging to the Vth Dynasty is the only one that is at all likely to have been the origin of this fine Cretan capital. Again a vase with two handles from Knossos is certainly an exact copy in local stone, of the regular Egyptian type of the Old Kingdom, which was quite unknown later. And two pieces of the brims of bowls, one of Egyptian diorite, the other of liparite, are of exactly the type made in the close of the IIIrd Dynasty at Medum, and in the early IVth Dynasty at Gizeh; this might perhaps last until the Vth Dynasty, but we could not suppose it to come later, as it would have been quite out of the run of later forms. The copying of motives and forms which passed entirely out of use, is a strong form of evidence; a single object might survive to later times, but for a form to be copied it must be the familiar and usual form at the time when the copy is made. Hence we cannot place the familiarity with these Egyptian types in Crete later than the Vth or perhaps IVth Dynasty.

Still earlier, the Western influence on Egypt is seen by the black incised bowls, of which one piece was found inside a mastaba of the time of Sneferu (end of IIIrd Dynasty), and another piece between

two mastabas of about the same age at Dendereh,
where it must have been buried in sand at the
period of the building. Another piece of such
black incised pottery was found in the tomb of
King Zer of the Ist Dynasty ; see Fig. 61.

This brings us back to a surprising series of
pieces of painted pottery from the Royal Tombs of
Ist Dynasty, the Ist Dynasty (Fig. 63). The forms
Aegean.   are Aegean ; the material, the facing, the
colouring, the varieties of pattern, all belong dis-
tinctively to the Aegean. The opinion of Professors
Furtwängler and Wolters is that these belong to the
earliest type of Island pottery. Certainly there is
nothing like them found in Egypt, except the
confessedly Aegean pottery of later times. One
prehistoric Egyptian vase has been compared with
them, but it has no resemblance in form, material,
facing, or colouring, and only an approximation to
one of the patterns. They stand unquestionably in
line with other Aegean ware. These pieces are
found scattered in several of the Royal Tombs ; and
those from the earlier tombs are of an earlier style.
Thus there is no absolute proof, but only a strong
presumption, that these belong to the age of the
tombs of the Ist Dynasty.

Further evidence is, however, given by a portion
of the original tomb offerings of King Zer, which
were left untouched by all the plunderers and
destroyers. In one corner-chamber of his tomb
were an alabaster vase of regular Ist Dynasty type,
four pottery jars of the same age, and nine jars of
foreign ware, different in forms, in material, and in
facing, from any Egyptian pottery of that age, but

agreeing in all these characteristics with Aegean pottery, and including a vase of the same nature as the painted pottery, but without decoration. The whole group was cemented together by the burning of the unguents which had been buried in the jars.

Here is then a case like that of the Kamares

FIG. 63.—Pottery of earliest Aegean style.   From Royal Tombs of the
Ist Dynasty, Egypt.

pottery at Kahun. The evidence is clear, there is no visible loophole for avoiding the archaeological conclusion. And the only argument against it is that no such pottery has been found in Greece, but only more advanced styles of such fabric under later conditions. Now that the Knossos finds have led all those who see their value to grant a connection in the IIIrd or IVth Dynasty, we may soon see the fighting frontier pushed over to include this great and distinctive group of the early Ist Dynasty.

Nor does this stand alone.   This year another class of foreign pottery has been found in the ruins

Ist Dynasty,
Cretan.

of the temple of Abydos, of the Ist Dynasty, and perhaps somewhat before it (Fig. 64).   The material is unlike any in Egypt, a dense black pottery ; the facing of it is usually highly burnished, unlike Egyptian of that age ; the forms are wholly un‑Egyptian, the long pointed amphora with curved neck, and the hollow feet to vases, being unmistakably of the Greek family.   Exactly similar pottery in material and finish, is found in fragments of the later Neolithic period at Knossos ; a piece from Egypt and one from Knossos when seen side by side seem as if they had been broken from the same jar.   The forms of the Cretan examples are not yet re‑established, but some at least are the same as the Egyptian examples.   As most of the

FIG. 64.—Polished black pottery of Cretan origin. Temple of Abydos.   Dyn. I.

cups of this type at Abydos had contained a brilliant red haematite paint, it is very likely that the pottery came over as vehicles for trade products.

Yet again in the Ist Dynasty deposit of ivory and glazed objects in the temple of Abydos, was a cast copper figure of foreign style which is of the same family as the copper figures found in the Diktaean cave.

And all this leads us back to the Egyptian pre-historic age. There we see commonly painted on the pottery, and on walls of a tomb, the large ships then in use. Some had as *Prehistoric.* many as 60 oars, yet we see the greatest of the Venetian fighting galleys had only 24 on a side. A rowing ship is useless on the Nile, except for sometimes getting down stream, as no rowing would suffice to take a large vessel continuously up against the current. But the rowing galley has been the vessel of the Mediterranean, from the French navy back to the Phoenician, and no one knows how long before. These great vessels, which bore various ensigns showing the ports from which they started, must have been concerned in important business ; probably trading the oil and skins and wood one way, and the dates and corn of Egypt in return. Among their imports were probably the foreign bowls of black incised ware, filled in with white, which are found even as far back as near the beginning of the prehistoric civilisation. They clearly belong to that foreign class which is found as far apart as Spain, Bosnia, and Troy ; and the original home of this pottery has yet to be found, in that Mediterranean region about which we are just beginning to discover our own ignorance.

If at present our evidence of connection between Egypt and the West, before the XIIth Dynasty, rests upon the identity of styles and fabrics, we must remember how that same class of evidence in later periods has been amply reinforced by dated objects with inscriptions, found in most unequivocal positions. And we may then at last reach the conception that after all, civilisation started at much the same time all round the Mediterranean, but advanced rather sooner in Egypt than on the northern shores.

In this study of the facts which link together the early history of Europe with that of Egypt, we have now seen the varied sources and values of the different kinds of archaeological evidence ; and the modes by which the accumulation of different evidences may reinforce the conclusions, and render them more exact.

CHAPTER XIII

THE ETHICS OF ARCHAEOLOGY

AT first sight, ethics might not seem to have more to do with archaeology than with chemistry or astronomy. Yet even in those subjects *Individual* an entire monopoly of some useful *rights.* material, or the destruction of the only records of irreplaceable observations, would bring in serious questions of individual right. It is notorious what a large element of conduct is involved in biology, where species are being destroyed every year, where the rabbit and the thistle have been wantonly made the curse of a continent, and where a mixture is taking place which will efface the results of ages of segregation. In archaeology there is perhaps a greater range of ethical questions, of the individual *versus* the community, than in any other science. And the results of action are the more serious as the material is very limited, and perhaps no other chance of observation may ever occur. In most sciences the opportunity of experiment and observation is unlimited. If an alloy is spoiled it can be remade at once, if a star is not examined to-night it may be next night, if a plant is not grown this year it

may be next year.   But Theodoric's gold armour
once melted, we shall never know what it was like ;
the heads of the Parthenon statues once burnt to
lime, are gone for ever ; or the Turin papyrus once
broken up, we can hardly hope ever to recover all
the history it contained.

The destruction that has gone on, and is now
going on continuously, seems as if it could leave
scarcely anything for the information of
future ages.   Every year sees wiped out
the remains which have lasted for thousands of years
past.   Now, in our own day, the antiquities of South
Africa and of Central and South America have been
destroyed as rapidly as they can be found.   Elsewhere, engineers of every nation use up buildings as
quarries or wreck them for the sake of temporary
profit, or for more legitimate purposes as in the
submersion of Philae and Nubia.   Speculators, native
and European, tear to pieces every tomb they can
find in the East, and sell the few showy proceeds
that have thus lost their meaning and their history.
Governments set commissioners to look after things,
who leave the antiquities to be plundered while they
are living in useless ease.   And the casual discoveries
that are made perish in a ghastly manner.   The
Saxon regalia of Harold, the treasures of Thomas
à Becket's shrine, the burial of Alfred, the burial of
Theodoric, and the summer palace of Pekin, have
within modern memory all gone the same way as
the wonders that perished in the French sack of
Rome or the Greek sack of Persia.   However we
may deplore this, our present consideration is destruction by archaeologists, and what their responsibilities

are in difficult situations. In all ages there has
been destruction for gold and valuables, and in the
Renascence a ruthless seizure of marbles and stone
work. To that succeeded destruction for the sake
of art, excavations in which everything was wrecked
for the chance of finding a beautiful statue. Then
in the last generation or two, inscriptions became
valued, and temple sites in Greece and in Egypt,
and palaces in Babylonia, have been turned over,
and nothing saved except a stone or a tablet which
was inscribed. At last a few people are beginning
to see that history is far wider than any one of these
former aims, and that, if ever we are to understand
the past, every fragment from it must be studied and
made to tell all it can.

But still there continues the plundering of sites
in the interest of show museums, where display is
thought of before knowledge, as is unhappily the
case in many national collections. To secure an
attractive specimen, a tomb will be wrecked, a wall
destroyed, a temple dragged to pieces and its history
lost, a cemetery cleared out with no record of its
burials. And when carefully authenticated and recorded specimens reach museums, their fate is not
yet a safe one, especially in local museums. Stones
will be built into walls, and ruined by the damp
bringing salt out; objects are left to drop to pieces
from lack of chemical knowledge, or from the official
dread of the responsibility of doing right instead of
allowing wrong. Information is deliberately destroyed; labels are thrown away or heaped together
out of the way in a glass case where the objects are
artistically displayed, with no more history than if

they had come from a dealer. Groups of things, whose whole value consists in their collocation as they were found, are scattered up and down a museum as if they had no meaning. Or priceless antiquities will be left out for years of exposure to weather, as certain sculptures were in London, until at last they received worthy safeguarding in defiance of the Treasury. Unhappily far too many of those who are responsible for keeping the things which have at last reached a haven, need educating in the elements of their profession.

This leads to another difficult question, that of restoration. The horrible destruction which has
Restoration. gone on under that term is now somewhat recognised, after much, or most, of the original buildings of our ancestors have disappeared beneath scraping and recutting, so that we only possess a copy of what has been. And in museums till within the last few years, statues were so elaborately built up out of what was—or was not —to be had, that it is often a difficult preliminary study to set aside the shams. In the Louvre there is the honesty of stating how much has been added to the original; and the list is sometimes so long that it is hard to make out what gave the first idea to the restorer for building up his work. Yet in many cases some mere supports are needful, and the best museums now make such helps as distinct as possible from the original. The only full solution of the matter is the great extension of the use of casts; and the ideal museum of sculpture would have the originals untouched on one side of a gallery,

and the full restoration of casts of the same things
on the other side.

When we stand face to face with a problem like
that of the Forum at Rome there rise a multitude
of questions which have intricate and
far-reaching solutions. The removal of Sacrifices.
the latest of the pavements of the Forum has been
bitterly resented. The Sacred Way is gone, and
what is there for sentiment to dwell on ! Yet who
would reasonably prefer the Lower Empire to the
Twelve Caesars ? And then is not the Republic
still more interesting and less known ? And then
the Kings hold a prerogative of glamour to every
schoolboy ; and what was Rome before the Kings ?
We see the inevitable result of such a crowd of
interests, in the honeycomb of pits and planks and
tunnels and iron girders which now bewilder the
visitor, where formerly he walked down the Sacred
Way and blessed his soul in romantic peace.

Now this elaborate treatment is most desirable,
but is scarcely attainable unless there is a strong
public interest, and a government willing to carry
out proper conservation. Let us turn to a different
set of conditions, as at the temple of Osiris at
Abydos. There were more than a dozen different
levels of building ; all the lower ones only of mud
brick ; the whole of the lower levels under the high
Nile, and certain to be a mud swamp so soon as the
Nile rose next summer. To treat such a place like
the Forum would have involved enormous iron
substructure layer under layer, and a wide drying
area for hundreds of yards around, at a cost of certainly five figures. No one would be likely to give

a hundredth of the cost to attain that end.   If any part were left without clearing to the bottom, the next high Nile would make entire pudding of it. And so the permanent preservation of such a site was impossible.   All that could be done whenever it was begun, was to dig it in as dry a season as possible, when the water was at its lowest ; to clear it entirely to water level ; and to make plans, levelling, and records, of every wall and every detail, removing everything that stood in the way of going lower.   Henceforward that temple site, instead of existing in unseen layers of solid earth, exists only on paper.

Now here is a great responsibility.   Whatever is not done in such an excavation can never be done. Responsibility.   The site is gone for ever ; and who knows what further interests and new points of research may be thought of in future, which ought to have received attention.   Are we justified morally in thus destroying a temple site, a cemetery, a town, while we may feel certain that others would see more in it in future ?   If a site would continue un-touched, and always equally open to research, it would be wrong to exhaust such places.   But what are the conditions ?   In Egypt sites are continually passing under cultivation, and once cultivated no one would ever know more about them.   They are being continually dug away for earth to spread on the fields, and all that lies in them is scattered and lost. The stonework is continually the prey of engineers and lime-burners.   The Nile is always rising, so that every few centuries makes ground inaccessible that was previously out of water.   And the probable movement of invention and appliances will most likely bring under cultivation in future most of the cemetery sites which are now bare desert. In the last few years most of the cemetery and temple sites of Nubia have been blotted out by the new lake for irrigation. Further, on any site of cemetery, temple, or town which is known to contain anything, the native will dig by night if he cannot do so by day, and will leave nothing but a wreck behind. It is sadly unlikely that there will be anything left to excavate in Egypt a century hence ; all the known sites will be exhausted in twenty years more at the present rate. A thousand years hence—a trifle in the history of Egypt—people will look back on these present generations as the golden days when discoveries came thickly year by year, and when there was always something to be found. And therefore the best thing that can be done under all these conditions is to work with the fullest care and detail in recording, to publish everything fully, and to then trust the history of Egypt to a few hundred copies of books instead of to solid walls and hidden cemeteries. The destruction which is needful to attain knowledge is justified if the fullest knowledge is obtained by it, and if that is so safely recorded that it will not again be lost. The only test of right is the procuring the greatest amount of knowledge now and in future.

Here we are landed in a question on which very different positions are taken. What are the rights of the future ? Why should we limit Rights of the our action, or our immediate benefit or future. interest, for the sake of the future? If ever this question comes into practical dealings, it does so in historical work.   Any one who is above the immediate consideration of food and starvation, does consider the future.   Our public buildings are preserved for the use of coming generations ; our libraries and museums are largely for the benefit of those yet unborn.   Was not the future of England the great charge, the inspiring aim of Alfred, of Edward I, of William III ?   Do we not even now spend ungrudgingly for the great future of our colonies?   In every direction we unquestioningly assume that the future has its rights ; that distant generations of our own flesh and blood are far more to us than present millions of other races ; that the knowledge, the possessions, the aims, that we have inherited are but a trust to be passed on to the nation yet to be.

And to those who live not only in the present but also in past ages by insight and association, the transitory stewardship of things becomes the only view possible.   In this generation I possess a gem, a scarab, a carving : it is almost indestructible, it may be lost for a time but will reappear again a thousand, five thousand, twenty thousand years hence in some one else's hands, and be again a delight and a revelation of past thought, as it is to-day.   We have no right to destroy or suppress what happens just for the present to be in our power.   To do so is to take the position of a Vandal in the sack of Rome.

The past also has its rights, though statues may be misappropriated and churches be " restored."
Rights of the past. A work that has cost days, weeks, or years of toil has a right to existence. To murder a man a week before his time we call a

crime ; what are we to call the murder of years of
his labour ?   Or, without touching life, what difference
is there between putting a man in prison for a year
so that he cannot work, and destroying a year's work
when it is done ?   If anything, the balance is in
favour of preventing rather than destroying his
work.   Every monument we see has been lovingly
intended, carefully carved, piously erected, in hopes
that it would last.   And who are we to defeat all
that thought and labour ?   Every tablet, every little
scarab, is a portion of life solidified ;—so much will,
so much labour, so much living reality.   When we
look closely into the work we seem almost to watch
the hand that did it ; this stone is a day, a week, of
the life of some living man.   I know his mind, his
feeling, by what he has thought and done on this
stone.   I live with him in looking into his work, and
admiring, and valuing it.   Shall I then turn on him
like a wild beast and kill so much of his life ?
Surely if we would draw back from wiping out a few
years of the life of some man with whom we have no
sympathies, far more should we shrink from even
hurting the beautiful and cherished result of the life
of a man whose mind we admire and honour in his
work.   I give my life to do so much work in it, and
if I were to know that every night the work of the
day would be annihilated, I had rather be relieved of
the trouble of living.   In all worth, in all realness,
the life of past men preserved to us has rights as
veritably as the life of present men.

The work of the archaeologist is to save lives ;
to go to some senseless mound of earth, some hidden
cemetery, and thence bring into the comradeship of

N

man some portions of the lives of this sculptor, of that artist, of the other scribe ; to make their labour familiar to us as a friend ; to resuscitate them again, and make them to live in the thoughts, the imaginations, the longing, of living men and women ; to place so much of their living personality current side by side with our own labours and our own thoughts. And has not the past its rights, as well as the present and the future ?

What care then, what conscience, must be put into the work of preserving as much as possible of the past lives which those about us are wishing to know and to share in. The mummy of Rameses or of Thothmes, the portrait of the builder of the great pyramid (Fig. 65), or of the Pharaoh of the Exodus (Fig. 66) is a permanent mental possession of all cultivated mankind, as long as our literature shall last. The knowledge of the growth of the great civilisation of Egypt, from the days of men clad in goat-skins to the height of its power, has all been reconstructed in the past ten years, and will be part of the common stock of our knowledge of man, so long as civilisation continues.

With the responsibilities before us of saving and caring for this past life of mankind, what must be
Duties.   our ethical view of the rights and duties of an archaeologist ? Conservation must be his first duty, and where needful even destruction of the less important in order to conserve the more important. To uncover a monument, and leave it to perish by exposure or by plundering, to destroy thus what has lasted for thousands of years and might last for thousands to come, is a crime. Yet

Fig. 65. The Builder of
the Great Pyramid.

Fig. 66. The Pharaoh of
the Exodus.

it is the incessant failing of the thoughtless amateur, who knows nothing of the business ; and far too often also the inexcusable malpractice of those who know better. To wantonly destroy a monument by cutting pieces out, whether to put them in a museum or to hide them in a pile of curiosities, is unjustifiable if the whole can be preserved entire. In the case of only fragments remaining, a selection often must be chosen ; yet even then copies of the whole of the material should be made and published all together. To unearth whole tombs or chambers full of objects, whether in an Egyptian cemetery or a Roman camp, and neglect to record and publish the facts of the position or groups of the objects, should debar the inefficient explorer from ever touching such places again. To remove things without ascertaining all that is possible about their age, meaning, and connections, is as inexcusable as it is easy. To undertake excavating, and so take the responsibilities for preserving a multitude of delicate and valuable things, unless one is prepared to deal with them efficiently, both mechanically and chemically, is like undertaking a surgical operation in ignorance of anatomy. To turn over a site without making any plans, or recording the positions and relations of things, may be plundering, but it is not archaeology. To remove and preserve only the pretty and interesting pieces, and leave the rest behind unnoticed, and separated from what gave them a value and a meaning, proves the spirit of a dealer and not that of a scholar. To leave a site merely plundered, without any attempt to work out its history, to see the meaning of the remains found, or to publish what may serve future students of the place or the subject, is to throw away the opportunities which have been snatched from those who might have used them properly.

To suppose that excavating—one of the affairs which needs the widest knowledge—can be taken up by persons who are ignorant of most or all of the technical requirements, is a fatuity which has led, and still leads, to the most miserable catastrophes. Far better let things lie a few centuries longer under the ground, if they can be let alone, than repeat the vandalisms of past ages without the excuse of being a barbarian.

We must always have regard to what may be the condition of sites and of knowledge five hundred or *Future of Museums.* five thousand years hence. For if you will deal with thousands of years you must take thousands of years into account. If a site is certain to be destroyed by natural causes, or the cupidity of man, then an imperfect examination and a defective record of it is better than none. But to ensure the fullest knowledge, and the most complete preservation of things, in the long run, should be the real aim. To raid the whole of past ages, and put all that we think effective into museums, is only to ensure that such things will perish in course of time. A museum is only a temporary place. There is not one storehouse in the world that has lasted a couple of thousand years. Only two or three bronze statues have come down to us from classical times preserved by each generation. A few pieces of gold work have been treasured for a little over a thousand years, but only in North

Italy. And the whole of our present active clearance of things, that have hitherto lasted safe underground for six thousand years or more, practically ensures that they shall not last one thousand longer. The gold work will be the first thing to disappear, as it is even now disappearing every few years from museums into the melting-pot. And it is a serious question whether we are morally justified in thus ensuring its destruction by exposure. As a counsel of perfection I should like to see twenty electrotypes made of every bit of ancient gold and silver work, and these dispersed over all countries. It might then be considered whether it would not be a noble act to bury the whole of the gold where it would cost a national undertaking to recover it, say in a hundred fathoms of water, and so preserve it for future ages, when only a few wrecks of the electrotypes would have survived. The future of the rest of museum treasures cannot so certainly be anticipated. Bronze is sure to disappear in warfare sooner or later, especially as metals grow scarcer owing to exhaustion of mines. Ivories will probably vanish, like most fragile things, by mechanical damage. Pottery and vases will go the same way as the museum of Kertch, which was bashed to pieces by a disappointed European soldiery. Stone carving has a promise of longer life, especially if it is reused in buildings, and so saved from exposure and wear ; for instance, whenever the Baptistry of Pisa may fall to pieces, a mine of Latin inscriptions will come to light. But, broadly speaking, there is no likelihood that the majority of things now in museums will yet be preserved anything like as long as they have

already lasted.   The hordes of anarchy and of Asia
have never left Europe alone for more than a few
centuries.

It is then to the written record, and the published
illustrations, that the future will have mainly to look.
Our books will probably not last more
than a few hundred years ; and it will
be reprints of the most valued, and summaries of the
others that will be the sources of knowledge in the
future thousands.   The wide spread of publications
in different countries, which are never likely to all
undergo eclipses simultaneously, is the best guarantee
for the permanence of knowledge.   But by the time
the First Dynasty has doubled its age, we cannot
expect that the greater part of our record of it will
still be known.   Certainly the inefficient and incon-
clusive books will vanish first ; and the more compact
and generally used a work is, the longer are its
chances of life. We must always remember therefore
that in archaeological work we are removing what
would be as solid proof to future ages as it is now to
us ; and we are trusting all future knowledge of the
facts to inflammable paper, and the goodwill of
successive generations, many of whom may have
very different interests.   Had any past age of civilisation dug up and removed every trace of the earlier
times, and committed all the results to their literature,
we should not be able to learn anything but some
brief summary, nor glean but a few trifling fragments,
which would have lost their meaning and connection.

And here we come against another large ethical
question of the rights of the individual against the
community, in the claim made by the state to

interfere with property in antiquities, in ways in which it does not interfere with any other property. From past ages the **State Claims.** English law has claimed for the Crown all treasure accidentally discovered. Such a law is the best way to ensure that no such discoveries are made known, and to drive the finder to put all such treasures in the melting pot. The actual gain to the Crown is ignorably trivial, certainly not an average of a thousand pounds a year ; yet, in order to grab this trifle, the law drove all such treasures to destruction. At last an improvement was made by the Crown only demanding specimens needed for the national collection, and paying intrinsic value for them. Even some old candlesticks, the proceeds of an XVIIIth century burglary, were claimed when accidentally found.

And when the state does not claim, the landlord or tenant makes a claim, which is just as bad, as such claims lead workmen always to conceal and sell surreptitiously the antiquities which are continually found in all working in old towns. The only law which could act for the full preservation of antiquities would be the grant of the entire rights to the finder if he proclaims his find, but no rights in what he does not proclaim. The actual average gains of an average landlord *per annum* by discoveries of antiquities are at present incalculably small, probably not a farthing in the pound on the rental or anything near that. Hence there would be no perceptible loss by granting finds to the finder ; and everything would be saved and preserved as it was found. At least a beginning could be made by landlords and public bodies offering full intrinsic value for any gold and silver found on their premises ; they could not lose by that, and they might gain large profits in the archaeological value of things.   To suppose that (without great precautions) they can get the whole value of finds by simply claiming them, is fatuous.

This same fatuous idea pervades many governments.   It is thought that by simply making a law, digging can be prevented, or antiquities can be kept in a country.   Such laws merely enforce an extensive illicit system, through which valuable and important things can readily be removed in defiance of law, whenever they are found.   There is not a country from which any antiquity could not be removed by sufficient care in smuggling.   Every national museum has its underground feeders, knows how to defeat the laws of other countries, and incessantly grows in spite of laws.   To seize property without paying its real value is seldom a profitable proceeding in the long run, and that is what every government tries to do with antiquities.   The Italian government has confiscated a large part of the values of private collections, by forbidding the exportation of any important picture or statue.   And yet such things can and do leave Italy.   The Greek government, as well as the Turkish, forbid the exportation of any and every kind of antiquity ; yet fine things from both lands continually come over to the West.

These confiscatory laws, these claims on private property on behalf of the state, are more or less illogical nibblings on a wide claim which no state has ventured yet to formulate, —namely, that all objects of past generations are

State Rights.

public property. This means, if fully carried out, that no person can own any object of antiquity as private property. No private collections would be possible in such a condition, all would belong to the state. Of course there is a huge amount of material which is duplicate, and not needed in a national collection ; but the state claims would be maintained if all collections must be placed in a public building, (such as a local museum) where they could be seen. The energy of collectors, the transfer of specimens from one to another, would not be stopped, only the objects would be compulsorily visible in a public place. And everything wanted for a national collection would be transferred. This condition of things is slowly being reached by the state buying important objects continually, when they are sold on changing hands. But the logical outcome of the present laws and present tendency would be this nationalisation of all antiquities. Whether such a result would be satisfactory at all points may be doubted ; but it is clearly a position to which all changes at present tend. If fully and honourably carried out by the state paying the finder full value for all it took, and giving up confiscation of all sorts, the result would probably be the best that could happen for archaeology.

One great result of defining the position thus, would be to prevent any ancient buildings being destroyed or altered without state consent. If every structure, say, over five hundred years old, needed three months' notice to an inspector before it could be pulled down or dealt with, there would be a great check on the present changes. Every cathedral and church, every castle and manor-house, would need special licence for changes in all parts older than the prescribed limit. A notice of one week might be required for the destruction of structures as yet not known, which were unearthed in course of digging. Such a protection of monuments would not affect vested interests or property values nearly as much as an ordinary railway bill that passes through Parliament without a protest ; and it seems not too much to hope that such a protection of all monuments of historic interest might be carried out. The legal position might take the form of pronouncing all ancient buildings, stone circles, and earthworks the ultimate property of the Crown, with the existing owners having full powers as trustees for the Crown to preserve, use, and enjoy such property, and to sell or devise such trusteeship in every way as if the property was not beyond the age limit of private property. Only the right of destruction and alteration would be reserved.

A state register of works of art is desired by Professor Ernest Gardner, who proposes that (1) the ownership of works of ancient art and sculptures and pictures by great masters should be entered on a register in charge of a public registrar ; (2) the registrar should have a right to see to the safety of such objects ; (3) any fairly qualified scholar may apply to be entered on a register of students kept by the registrar ; (4) owners of registered works must fix times for exhibition to students or to the public, or else a registered student must be allowed to see any work within a reasonable period ; (5) the owner, if absent, must appoint some one to preserve and exhibit such works ; (6) in case of sale of a work to a foreign country, the government shall have the option of retaining it at the price fixed for the sale.

The attitude of foreign governments regarding scientific excavating has not been happy. Too often the prohibitions have been used Excavating not in the interests of archaeology, but Laws. for promoting plundering. Because it is easy to drop on an open excavation, all regular excavations have been fenced with severe difficulties and costs ; while in Greece and Turkey none of the proceeds have been allowed to the finder. On the other hand, it is difficult to always drop on a surreptitious native, and the sympathy of the courts—in Egypt at least—is openly on the side of the plundering native, who is seldom punished for anything. Hence the curious situation is that the whole values of the property have been solely created by the labours and study of the archaeologist; yet he is almost debarred from using the material which an ignorant peasant may dig and destroy as he pleases.

The form of law which is wanted is (1) the punishment of all destruction or removal of antiquities, by a special court, independent of local sympathies or favouring of the plunderer ; (2) the rigid requirement of technical knowledge and ability in those who excavate, with the condition that everything is published promptly, and that nothing found can be sold or pass except into a public museum ; (3) the right of the government of each country to such objects as are necessary to the national collection, on reimbursing whatever may have been given as bakhshish to the finder, and some proportion of the costs according to the case.

CHAPTER XIV

THE FASCINATION OF HISTORY

THE love of past times, the craving for that which is gone, is one of the more obscure instincts which appears to be brought forward by the wider growth of interests of the mind. It takes many forms ; it appeals to the intellect, to the curiosity, to the affections ; yet it is really a single instinct, and one which, from its strength, must spring from a primal cause.

The sense of loss touches us at every sunset, and in anticipation tinges all the afternoon with the sense of lengthening shadows. Even the things that seem most common, least worthy, when in use, all gain some being as time passes. Each little thing, that carelessly we value not at first, grows rich with store of years. As Antony says—

> You all do know this mantle : I remember
> The first time ever Caesar put it on ;
> 'Twas on a summer's evening in his tent,
> That day he overcame the Nervii.

Still more do places gain their hold upon us, unheeded at the time. A store of memories of days spent amid strong associations, that stirred and built the mind, are the truest riches in all after-life.   We dwell upon those portions of the past, those days at Athens, or Florence, or in the Forum, as on a treasure ; they are a portion of our life crystallised into the structure of our thoughts—a haven of the imagination.

And how much deeper still is the sense of the past when we turn to friends,—or even closer yet. One whom perhaps we hardly heeded in our daily life, is dignified at once by the irrevocable.   But all this is merely our personal regret : the direct, selfish, individual interest.

> But the tender grace of a day that is dead
> Will never come back to me.

Let us step from this out into the past beyond our personal touch.   See now a churchyard, tall in grass, with the dial on its stand, which each genera-tion has passed by—how full of memories of gone years it is, how the eye clings to its weathered disc and minds that so it was on the day of Trafalgar or the Boyne ; while by its side is the old carved sarcophagus tomb of some Turkey merchant, silently showing his virtues to each changing time, and calming the mind with quiet age.   We love such for the sake of the past, which draws us to its bosom to make one more link in the long chain.

And pass inside the church, where Tudor and Edwardian, and Norman and Saxon, have each poured out their souls ; in which every stone seems saturated with their longings ; where pleadings and rejoicings seem to mutely fill the dead air ; where the walls have echoed every bride and every infant

and every mourner through all the changing generations ; where *Fæder ure* has yielded to *pater noster*
before even our familiar supplications were ever
heard.   This indeed holds us as if it were a place
where we can actually live with the past selves that
have made us, and be at one with those who would
have craved to see us in the ages beyond them.

And if past loves and hopes seem thus to give
their life to the lasting walls, how fearful is the
breath of terror that clings round every stone of the
Colosseum.   One single mangled death there made
ten thousand fiends of men who sat on those benches ;
and every year had its thousands of such agonies,
through all the centuries.   The mass of horror
beyond all thought that dwells in that arena, is only
exceeded by the thousandfold fire of cruelty that
has burnt on those seats around.   The place is hell
petrified.

And, within a stone's throw of that, how the
whole past, from which our present ages have sprung,
lives before us in the Forum.   The triumphs where
the beauty of Greek art served but to make the clumsy
westerner gape ; where the noblest blood of other
lands, — Perseus, Caractacus, Zenobia,—has stood
abased ; where the barbaric Goth has fiercely joyed
in splendid pillage of its wondrous wealth ; where
Theodoric and Karl had each hoped to restore the
shattered decay, with the rough material of their own
kin, which needed yet a thousand years of hewing ;
a space of greater hopes and dreads, greater successes
and failures, than any other acre that we know.

And yet, before all this, there passed age after
age of men, who built up civilisations which we

just begin to perceive. The golden splendour of Mykenae, the earlier magnificence of Minoan Knossos, the delicate wares of still older Crete, all live with the same life as ourselves, all are precious to us as if we had made them, all make us fellow minds with those who thought and fashioned and treasured such things in like manner to ourselves.

Turn now to our own land, and on a wide western moor stand within a ring of grey stones, which our own flesh and blood there placed in faith and trust, for something greater than the cares of daily life ; so far from us in generations, so far from us in thoughts, that we can hardly grasp the pulse of the same life with them, and feel what they felt. Yet it draws us like those sounds which were the first music to man, the sough of the wind in the wood, and the lap of the wave on the shore, ever the sweetest yet to ourselves. And the grey stones still touch us and bind our thoughts and our love of all our forefathers to themselves in elemental memories.

What underlies all this fascination of the past? What is it that thus moves men

In thinking of the days that are no more?

It is the same great attraction, whether it be a personal memory, or the being of our forefathers, or a page strong with past life in some history, or the handling of the drinking bowls of the oldest kings of the earth as they come from the dust of Egypt. It is but one sense in varied forms. It is the love of life.

In primal seas first sprang that love of life,—of preservation, of continuity of life. Even long before man it led to the moral growth of self-sacrifice, of affection, of social union. In man it led the Stoic on to the brotherhood of all men, and the responsibility of man for man. It has led the modern forward to the brotherhood of all existing life, the responsibility for the animal as well as the man. It now leads us on to clinging to the life of our ancestors, their being, and their natures ; and beyond that to the fascination of all history, as being the continuity of life, the ever-shifting changes of the one great chain which we see around us at its present stage, and of which we form part. The man who knows and dwells in history adds a new dimension to his existence ; he no longer lives in the one plane of present ways and thoughts, he lives in the whole space of life, past, present, and dimly future. He sees the present narrow line of existence, momentarily fluctuating, as one stage, like innumerable other stages that have each been the all-important present to the short-sighted people of their own day. He values the present as the most complete age of history for study, as explaining the past. He values the past as the long continuity that has brought about the result of the present, in which he happens to breathe. He lives in all time ; the ages are his, all live alike to him ; the present is not more real than the past, any more than the room in which he sits is more real than the rest of the world. Cleaving to that one stream of life which branch by branch has flowed through so many channels in all the ages, and still runs on into the future, he can give account of the Fascination of History.

INDEX

Glycerine 91
Glycin 83
Gold collar from Enkomi 154
,, foil 67-68, 98
,, pin, Cypriote 155
,, preservation of 180-181
,, treatment of 98
,, value offered for 184
Governments, attitude of 183, 187
Graeco-Egyptian vases 144
Graffiti, copying 72
Grave, age of, by sequence-dates 129
,, dressing of 76-77
Greece, *see Europe*
,, conditions of work in 26, 32, 33
Greek pottery 17
,, workmen 26-27
Greeks in Egypt 142-144, 146
Grouping in museums 132
,, of objects as evidence 139
Groups in museums 172
,, numbering of 51
,, of ivories 91
,, of objects 48-49, 51, 69, 115, 172, 179
,, photographing of 80, 81
Guards to plates 116, 117
Gum, contraction of 93
Gurob 145, 148, 151, 152, 153, 156
Gutta-percha moulds 66

Haematite paint 166
Hammer dressing 105
,, light 99
,, sledge 112
Headings of plates 115
Head-lines of text 120
Head-shawls, seizure of 39
Helbeh 109
Heliogravure 119
Hinges 113
History, fascination of 189-193
,, importance of 4-5, 171, 193
,, knowledge of 4-5
Hibeh, El 9
Hissarlik, black incised ware 161, 167
Holes, excavated 43
,, in bricks 47
Hollow feet to vases 166
Hollows in ground 11, 12, 13, 44

Hollows in inscriptions 76
,, ,, packing 108
Hone-stone 113
Honesty in workmen 22, 34, 37
Horemheb 147
Horizontal position, photographing 80
Huts, mud, of excavators 6
Hypocephalus, bronze 76

Ialysos, tomb at 152
Idaean cave, bronze vases 155
,, ,, carved dish 155
Idleness, remedies for 21, 28
Illness among workmen 31, 37-38
Impressions of cylinders 66
Indestructibility of small antiquities 176
Index to books 120
India-rubber for dry-squeezing 63
Indications after rain 13
,, of nature of site 12, 13
Indices of types required 124
Infectious illness 38
Inking in of drawings 61, 63, 68
,, ,, ,, squeezes 61
Inks for drawing 52, 68
Ink-writing copied 72
,, ,, photographed 79
Inscriptions, columns and lines 72
,, copying 60-63, 72
,, ,, before removal 53
,, made legible 76
,, on stone 76
,, sanded 76
Insight in excavating 4-6
Inspectorship of antiquities 185
Instantaneous shutter 75
Instruments, use of 54-55
Inventory-sheets for small objects 69-70
Iron, treatment of 102
Ironing textiles 89
Irregularities in plates 115
Israel stele 62
Ivory, destruction of 181
,, preservation of 90-92
,, tablet of Zer 76

Jaw, removal for measurement 53
Jelly for extracting salt 89-90

INDEX

Skull, removal for measurement 52
Slate backing to frescoes 97
Sliding of earth 42
Slopes of rubbish-mounds 11
Smuggling of antiquities 184
Sneferu, black incised ware 163
Soaking of bronzes 101
,,   ,, iron 102
,,   ,, lead 102
,,   ,, pottery 88
,,   ,, stones 86
,,   ,, textiles 89
Softening in packing 106, 108-109
Sorting fragments 102-104
Spain, pottery from 159-160, 167
Speculators, destruction by 170
Spies 38-39
Spoke-brush, use of 60-61, 113
,,   shave 113
Square 113
Squareness on plates 115
Squares of plans 53
Squeezes, dry 61-63
,,   wet 60-61
Stain, ebony 68
State claims 182-184
,,   register of works of art 186-187
,,   rights 184-187
Stations, surveying 57-58
Statistical sorting of pottery 128
Statuary, casts of 172
,,   lighting of 131-132
,,   preservation of 180
,,   restoration of 172
Statuette, ebony 78
Stirrup vases 145, 146, 154
,,   ,, variation with age 153-154
Stone chips 9, 13
,,   of buildings 76
,,   vases, block-tints for 70
,,   ,, drawing from fragments 71
,,   ,, sorting fragments 102-104
Stones, large 30
,,   moving of 27
,,   salt in 86
,,   scale of drawing 69
Stops in manuscripts 120
,,   ,, photographing 74-75

Storing of antiquities 6
,,   ,, ropes 46
Straw for packing 108, 109, 112
Strings of beads 95-96
Stucco, coloured 88
,,   facing 87
,,   on bricks 96
,,   on walls 47
,,   on wood 96
Students' plates 119
Style, discrimination of 14, 17-18
Successive ages, classed 126
Super-heated wax for preserving 90
Superimposed buildings 41-42
Support, points of, in packing 105-106
Survey, three-point 56
Surveying 5, 53-59
,,   of walls 52
Survival of museums 180-181
,,   ,, things in use 128, 150
Systematic archaeology 122-135
,,   work in excavating 2
Systematizers needed 123

Tables, printing of 120
Tablet, ivory 76
Tahutmes II 151
,,   III 151, 152, 153
Tally for accounts 37-38
Tanis, with obelisks 9
,,   workers at 20
Tape-measure 55, 113
,,   steel- 55
Tapioca-water 55
Telescope used in work 28
Tell el Amarna, frescoes at 88
,,   ,,   ,, vases at 147, 148, 155, 156
,,   ,, Yehudiyeh, cemetery mounds 43
Temple, causes of ruin 10
,,   evidence of 47
,,   site, clearance of 41-47
,,   ,, nature of 9-10
Tenting in desert 6
Textiles 89
Theodolite 55
Thickness of lines in drawing 69
Threads 65, 90, 92, 95
Three-colour photography 119

208 INDEX

THE END

Printed by R. & R. CLARK, LIMITED, *Edinburgh.*

For EU product safety concerns, contact us at Calle de José Abascal, 56–1°,
28003 Madrid, Spain or eugpsr@cambridge.org.

www.ingramcontent.com/pod-product-compliance
Ingram Content Group UK Ltd.
Pitfield, Milton Keynes, MK11 3LW, UK
UKHW010343140625
459647UK00010B/795